FRAGMENTARY DECREES FROM THE ATHENIAN AGORA

Hesperia Supplements

The *Hesperia* Supplement series (ISSN 1064-1173) presents book-length studies in the fields of Greek archaeology, art, language, and history. Founded in 1937, the series was originally designed to accommodate extended essays too long for inclusion in the journal *Hesperia*. Since that date the Supplements have established a strong identity of their own, featuring single author monographs, excavation reports, and edited collections on topics of interest to researchers in classics, archaeology, art history, and Hellenic studies.

Hesperia Supplements are electronically archived in JSTOR (www.jstor.org), where all but the most recent titles may be found. For order information and a complete list of titles, see the ASCSA website (www.ascsa.edu.gr).

Hesperia Supplement 38

FRAGMENTARY DECREES FROM THE ATHENIAN AGORA

Michael B. Walbank

The American School of Classical Studies at Athens
2008

Cover illustration: Fragment of an honorific decree, Agora I 5771, 4th–3rd century B.C.

Library of Congress Cataloging-in-Publication Data

Walbank, Michael B., 1933–
Fragmentary decrees from the Athenian agora / Michael B. Walbank.
p. cm. — (Hesperia supplement ; 38)
Includes bibliographical references and indexes.
ISBN 978-0-87661-538-6 (alk. paper)
1. Agora (Athens, Greece) 2. Inscriptions, Greek—Greece—Athens. 3. Athens (Greece)—Antiquities. I. Title.
DF287.A23W35 2008
938′.5—dc22 2008029996

To the memory of

Benjamin Dean Meritt
1899–1989

and

Homer Armstrong Thompson
1906–2000

in gratitude and affection

PREFACE AND ACKNOWLEDGMENTS

I am deeply grateful to the late Homer A. Thompson, Director Emeritus of the Agora Excavations, and to the late Benjamin D. Meritt, who first assigned these fragments to me for study and publication. I am grateful, too, to John McK. Camp II, the current Field Director of the Agora Excavations, and to T. Leslie Shear Jr., the former Field Director, for granting me permission to work at the Agora over the past several years. I thank also Charalambos Kritzas, the former Director of the Epigraphic Museum in Athens, for permission granted to me in 2001 and 2002 to study documents held in that collection.

I am especially grateful to the late David M. Lewis, and to Geoffrey Woodhead and Stephen Lambert. Others who have helped me with their comments and suggestions on specific problems arising from this work are Sean Byrne, John Camp, Alan Henry, Angelos Matthaiou, Graham Oliver, Michael Osborne, Ronald Stroud, Stephen Tracy, and John Traill.

All photographs are courtesy of the Agora Excavations; my thanks to Craig Mauzy.

At the urging of the anonymous referees to whom this work was submitted, I have kept speculation and restoration to a minimum. I thank them for their comments and advice.

Five fragments whose *editiones principes* appear here were also published by Stephen V. Tracy in 2003.[1]

1. *AAM*, pp. 38, 45–46, no. 1 (**63**, fragment *b*); pp. 38, 46–48, no. 2 (**50**); pp. 68–69, no. 2 (**75**); pp. 90–93, no. 3 (**67**); and pp. 104–107, no. 1 (**39**).

CONTENTS

ILLUSTRATIONS

EDITORIAL SYMBOLS

The editorial symbols applied to these inscriptions follow those in Sterling Dow's *Conventions in Editing: A Suggested Reformulation of the Leiden System* (Durham 1969), with one exception.

[ ]	restoration
< >	editorial correction
( )	resolution of abbreviation
{ }	editorial deletion
Γ̣	ambiguous Greek letter
[. . . .]	lacuna of approximately four letters
[- - - -]	lacuna of unknown number of letters
⟦ ⟧	correction by inscriber

Unlike Dow, I use underlining to indicate the text of a new fragment.

The following designation is also used:

+	The original publication has been supplemented by a new fragment or there is a significant new reading or interpretation

The Texts

I here present the *editiones principes* of 108 fragments of inscriptions, comprising parts of 100 decrees of the Athenian body politic (and subdivisions of it), including some dealing with councillors and their officers (the subject of *Agora* XV), and some of those listing and honoring the young men *(epheboi)* who had completed their higher education and military training. Among these are found proxeny decrees, honorifics, and grants of citizenship.

Their appearance here is the result of my systematic attempt to identify and publish all the remaining unpublished inscription fragments deriving from excavations carried out in the Athenian Agora between 1931 and 1967. Not included is a large number of unpublished fragments of a decree or decrees concerned with the celebration of the Eleutheria Festival in the mid-2nd century B.C., which I shall publish separately in due course, both because the nature of the monuments from which they derive is, as yet, unclear, and because their inclusion here would severely unbalance this study.

The present work is intended to serve as a supplement to A. G. Woodhead, *Agora* XVI, *Inscriptions: The Decrees* (Princeton 1977), as well as to B. D. Meritt and J. S. Traill, *Agora* XV, *Inscriptions: The Athenian Councillors* (Princeton 1974), but it includes also two examples of ephebic decrees, a category not included in either *Agora* XV or *Agora* XVI.

This volume follows the same arrangement as *Agora* XVI, in which entries are arranged chronologically, by definite or most likely dates, without separation into different categories. The date range is from the beginning of the 4th century to the end of the 2nd century B.C. Each fragment is described by inventory number, marble type, and the date and place of its discovery, with reference to the standard grid of the Agora Excavations, if known. The physical condition, dimensions, letter height(s), and spacing on each fragment follow. All dimensions are given in meters.

After the basic Greek text, in which restorations are not attempted unless they form parts of accepted formulas, there is a line-by-line epigraphical commentary, in which individual letters are described, where necessary, and similarities to other, published inscriptions are noted, followed by a limited textual commentary, in which possible restorations are sometimes discussed, but speculation is avoided. Finally, the significance of each fragment is indicated, if any can be discerned, as well as possible links to other published decrees. Each fragment is accompanied by a photograph.

1 Fragment of a decree, possibly a proxeny decree — Fig. 1

I 6397. A fragment of a stele of Pentelic marble discovered on June 2, 1951, east of the East Building (P 14), in a Byzantine context. It is broken all around and on the back.

H. 0.114, W. 0.098, Th. 0.073; L.H. 0.01–0.012; stoich. hor. 0.019, vert. 0.0185.

Beginning of 4th century B.C. — Stoich.

[- -]
[- - - - - - - - - - .]Ị A[- - - - - - - - - -]
[- - - - - - - - - -]ΗΝΣΤ[- - - - - - - -]
[- - - - - - - - - -]ΝΑΙΟ[- - - - - - - -]
[- - - - - - - - - -][[Ι]]ΓΙẠ[- - - - - - -]
[- - - - - - - - - -]ΕΤẠ[- - - - - - - - -]
[- -]

Line 1: These letters are so faint as to be almost invisible, but, in a strong oblique light, the bottom of a central vertical and the horizontal and the lower parts of the diagonals of alpha are visible.

Line 4: The first iota is very deeply cut; a gamma was first inscribed here. To the right of the second iota, a deep triangular notch may be the apex of an alpha.

Line 5: The apex of alpha is preserved.

The hand is distinctive and inconsistent. Note the occasional "double-striking"; the way in which verticals seem to lean back; the rather wide alpha with sloping bar; gamma whose horizontal slopes slightly down; epsilon whose lower horizontals are longer than the upper one; inconsistency in the placing of iota; variations in the shape of nu; omicron a rounded polygon made from a series of short straight lines; sigma whose topmost diagonal is longer and flatter than the lowest one; and the way in which the horizontal of tau slopes down to the right. With the exception of gamma and sigma, the features of the script noted here, including its inconsistency, can be found also in *IG* II^2 13a, and especially in *IG* II^2 13b.[1] The letter height and the horizontal, but not the vertical, spacing are the same. Thus, this is unlikely to be yet another fragment of *IG* II^2 13+, but could derive from a copy of that decree.

Line 4: [τὸς Ἀχαιὸς τὸς Α][[ι]]γιᾶ̣[ς]? See *IG* II^2 13a, lines 3 and 8.
Line 5: [προξένος καὶ εὐεργ]έτα̣[ς]?

Figure 1. Fragment of a decree, possibly a proxeny decree (1)

2 Fragment of the treaty of alliance between the Athenians and the Kephallenians — Fig. 2

I 5368. A fragment of a stele of Pentelic marble discovered on March 29, 1938, northeast of the Church of the Hypapanti (T 21), in the wall of a bothros. Part of the left side may be preserved below the surface, though badly worn. Otherwise, it is broken all around. The back has been reworked, and is now flat, with a pattern of regular pockmarks, typical of Byzantine work.

H. 0.206, W. 0.158, Th. 0.072; L.H. 0.007–0.008; stoich. 0.012 (square).

1. *IG* II^2 13a is now joined with *IG* II^2 68 and Stroud 1971, pp. 149–150, no. 3; see *SEG* XL 54 (EM 6881 + 2624 + 12917). *IG* II^2 13b (EM 6881a) is a nonjoining fragment deriving from the bottom of this stele.

Figure 2. Fragment of the treaty of alliance between the Athenians and the Kephallenians (2)

373/2 B.C.? Stoich. 26

[- -]
[. . .6. . .]Α̣Θ̣[. . . . . .18. . . . .]
[. . .6. . .]γραψ[. . . . . . . .16. . . . .]
[. .5. .]ΣΟΥ̣ΣΟ̣[. . . . . . . .16. . . . .]
[. . κα]ὶ ἐσαγό[ντων? . . . . . .12. . . . . .]
[. . . .] ἐ⟦ξ⟧αγ⟦όν⟧[των? . . . . . .13. . . . . . .]
[. . . .] μέχρι Τ[. . . . . . . .16. . . . .]
[. . ἐς] τὸ λοιπ[ὸν . . . . . . .14. . . . . . .]
[. .5. .]ΕΣ δὲ [. . . . . . . .17. . . . .]
[. .5. .]Ο̣Σ ἐγ Κεφ̣[αλληνίαι? . . .6. . .]
[. . . τῶ]ν ἐπιμε[λητῶν . . . . .10. . . . .]
[. . .6. . . α]ὐτῶν [. . . . . . .15. . . . .]
[. . . .8. . . .]Η̣Τ̣[. . . . . . . .16. . . . .]
[- -]

Line 1: The lower parts of a right diagonal and of the curve of a circular letter survive.

Line 3: The tips of the diagonals of upsilon are preserved, but the vertical is obscured by deep weathering; the upper left curve of a circular letter is visible after the second sigma.

Line 5: In the second stoichos the mason inscribed a sigma and a xi on top of one another; the presence of a sigma in the similar phrase in the previous line suggests that here sigma was a mistake and xi the correction. Omicron and nu also seem to be corrections; originally alpha and gamma were inscribed here.

Line 9: The upper right curve of omicron and the right third of the loop of phi survive; the outlines of the other letters are visible, despite heavy weathering.

Line 12: The tops of the verticals of eta and the upper half of a tau or a zeta survive.

Script, spacing, and marble are identical with those of *Agora* XVI, no. 46.[2] The existence of this fragment is noted on p. 67 of *Agora* XVI.

Because of its thickness and the treatment of its back, this cannot, at first sight, be attributed to *Agora* XVI, no. 46. The back has been reworked, however, and what can be read in line 9 confirms that this fragment does, indeed, derive from the same stele, but without a join.

Line 2: [ἀνα]γραψ[άτω]? Cf. *Agora* XVI, no. 46, lines 24–25.

3 Fragment of a list of names (appended to a decree?) Fig. 3

I 3058. A fragment of a stele of Pentelic marble discovered on June 29, 1935, in the area of the northwest part of the Odeion (J–M 9–11), in a marble dump. The stipple-dressed left side and flat, rough-picked back are preserved, the pick marks made with short horizontal strokes. A drafted edge adjoins the face. The left margin is 0.015, and there is a vertical uninscribed space of 0.045 below line 7.

H. 0.302, W. 0.119, Th. 0.099; L.H. 0.008; stoich. 0.019 (square).

Ca. 390–370 B.C. Stoich.

[- - - - - - - - - - - - - - - - - - -]
[. .]ΜΑ[- - - - - - - - - - - - - - -]
[.]Σ̣ΙΑΔ[- - - - - - - - - - - - - -]
Η̣ΣΛΥΣ[- - - - - - - - - - - - - -]
ΟΣΕΥΑ̣[- - - - - - - - - - - - - -]
ΗΣΙΣΤ̣[- - - - - - - - - - - - - - -]
ΑΘΗΝ̣[- - - - - - - - - - - - - - -]
ΘΟΥΔ[- - - - - - - - - - - - - - -]
vacat

Line 1: The lower halves of these letters survive.

Line 2: The right tip of a lower diagonal, probably of a sigma, is preserved.

Line 3: The bases of the verticals of eta survive, but not the horizontal.

Line 4: In the fifth stoichos the stone breaks on the base of a left diagonal.

Line 5: The left tip of the horizontal of tau survives.

Line 6: The surface after the eta has been obliterated, except for the top part of a left vertical.

Straight strokes tend to curve slightly. Alpha, delta, and lambda are quite broad, the horizontal of alpha set low and slightly angled down to the right; the middle horizontal of epsilon is shorter than the other two, the upper shorter than the lower; eta is narrow; omicron and theta are quite round and slightly smaller than other letters; the angle between the upper diagonals of sigma is sharper than that between the lower, the outer diagonals longer than the inner, the lowest projecting slightly beyond the left apex; the vertical of upsilon is longer than its diagonals. The same characteristic hand is found in *IG* II² 96 (EM 6975), but with different spacing and letter sizes. This should provide an approximate date and possible context.

The size of the *vacat* below line 7 suggests that this fragment derives from the bottom of its stele; thus it may be a list of ambassadors or oath-takers, appended at the end of a decree.[3]

Line 1: [κατὰ τὰ δ|όγ]μα[τα],[4] [ὀ|νό]μα[τα], or part of a name?

Line 2: [Ἐρ|υ]σ̣ιάδ[ας]? Cf. *IG* II² 96, line 27.

2. *IG* II² 98 + Schweigert 1940, pp. 321–324, no. 33 (EM 2707 + I 4113). Photograph of *IG* II² 98 and I 4113, Schweigert 1940, p. 321.

3. For examples of such lists, cf. *IG* II² 34, 41, 175, 186, 280, and 2378; the fragment published in *ArchEph* (1963) 1965, pp. 151–153, is another such list, probably of the very early 4th century B.C.

4. Cf. *IG* II² 96, line 24, and *IG* II² 97, lines 22–23 and 34.

Figure 3. Fragment of a list of names (appended to a decree?) (3)

Line 4: Εὔα̣[ρχος]? Cf. *IG* II² 96, line 26.
Lines 4–5: [῾Ηγ]|ησίστ̣[ρατος]?
Line 6: A personal name, or the ethnic Ἀθην̣[αῖοι] or Ἀθην̣[αίων]?

4 Fragment of the agreement between Athens and Troizen? Fig. 4

I 5405. A fragment of a stele of micaceous Pentelic marble discovered on April 19, 1938, at the Church of the Hypapanti, south of the Eleusinion (T 21), in a late context. It is broken all around and on the back. The inscribed face is polished.

H. 0.073, W. 0.045, Th. 0.054; L.H. 0.006; semi-stoich. hor. ca. 0.0085, vert. 0.0145.

Ca. 390–370 B.C. Semi-stoich.?

[- -]
[- - - - - - - - - -]Λ̣ΙΧ̣[- -]
[- - - - - - - - - -]ΤΑΥΤ̣[- -]
[- - - - - - - - - -]ΒΟΛ[- -]
[- -]

Figure 4. Fragment of the agreement between Athens and Troizen? (4)

Line 1: In the first stoichos the base of a steep right diagonal is visible; in the third the lower part of a less steep left diagonal is preserved. The different angles of these diagonals suggest the readings printed here.

Line 2: The left tip of the horizontal of tau survives.

The spacing and letter forms correspond to those of face A of *IG* II² 46+ (= *Agora* XVI, no. 35). Note particularly the tendency to double-strike certain letters, such as lambda and upsilon, and the angled bar of tau; letters are made with the same deep, small strokes. Note also the difference between the angles of the diagonals of triangular letters and those of chi.[5]

5 Fragments of the agreement between Athens and Stymphalos in Arkadia? Fig. 5

I 6384, I 4510a, I 4510b, I 2925. Four fragments of Pentelic marble may derive from the stele of *Agora* XVI, no. 47 (= *IG* II² 144+).[6] All share marble type and letter forms with *Agora* XVI, no. 47, and I believe that they are all fragments of that document.[7] Of these, fragment *a* may derive from face A; the other three fragments (*b, c,* and *d*) may derive from face B.

Fragment *a* (I 6384) was discovered on May 22, 1951, northeast of the Temple of Ares (L 7), in a Byzantine context. It is broken all around and on the back.

H. 0.065, W. 0.044, Th. 0.043; L.H. 0.009; stoich. hor. 0.0145, vert. 0.016.

Fragment *b* (I 4510a) was discovered on February 11, 1937, beneath Acropolis Street, east of the Post-Herulian Wall (T 24), in a context of very Late Roman times. It is broken all around and on the back.

H. 0.11, W. 0.10, Th. 0.052; L.H. 0.005–0.006; stoich. hor. 0.0125, vert. 0.0135.

Fragment *c* (I 4510b) was also discovered on February 11, 1937, but southeast of the Market Square, east of the Post-Herulian Wall (U 22), in a Byzantine context. It is broken all around and on the back.

H. 0.07, W. 0.067, Th. 0.063; L.H. 0.005–0.006; stoich. hor. 0.0125, vert. 0.0135.

Fragment *d* (I 2925) was discovered on May 25, 1935, east of the Middle Stoa (P 13), in a late context. It is broken all around and on the back. It was partly published in *Agora* XVI, pp. 67–68 and 70, where it was designated as fragment *r,* but without a text or a photograph.

H. 0.074, W. 0.048, Th. 0.043; L.H. 0.006–0.007; stoich. 0.013 (square).

Ca. 368 B.C.? Stoich.

Face A

a [- -]
[- - - - - - - -]E N[- - - - - - - - - - - - - - - - -]
[- - - - - - - -]ΞY[- - - - - - - - - - - - - - - - -]
[- - - - - - - - .]Δ[- - - - - - - - - - - - - - - - -]
[- - - - - - - - .]A[- - - - - - - - - - - - - - - - -]
[- -]

Line 1: Although the epsilon is set directly above the xi of line 2, the nu is placed well to the right of the upsilon of line 2; this raises the possibility that line 1 is more widely spaced and thus a heading of some sort.

5. Two other fragments of *IG* II² 46 were found in or close to the Agora: fragments *q,* I 4985, and *r,* I 5351 (Woodhead 1957, pp. 225–229, no. 85, and pls. 58, 59).

6. For photographs of all published fragments except *r,* I 2925, see Walbank 1986, pls. 71–76.

7. Five other fragments of *IG* II² 144 were found in or close to the Agora: *d,* I 2025 (Woodhead 1957, pp. 221–225, no. 84); *e,* I 5803; *g,* I 5751; *o,* I 5278 (Walbank 1986); and *r,* I 2925 (*Agora* XVI, pp. 67–68, 70).

Line 2: The right halves of the upper horizontals and the vertical of xi survive.

Ca. 368 B.C.? Stoich.

Face B

b

[- -]
[- - - - - - - . . .]Κ[- - - - - - - - - - - - - - - - - -]
[- - - - - - - . .]Λ̣ΑΧ[- - - - - - - - - - - - - - - - -]
[- - - - - - - .]ΑΝΤΡΙ̣[- - - - - - - - - - - - - - - -]
[- - - - - -]ΝΠΕΝΤ[- - - - - - - - - - - - - - - - -]
[- - - - - -]ΑΝΟΦ[- - - - - - - - - - - - - - - - - -]
[- - - - - - - .]ΕΓΡ̣[- - - - - - - - - - - - - - - - - -]
[- -]

c

[- -]
[- - - - - - - .]ΣΙ[- - - - - - - - - - - - - - - - - - -]
[- - - - - -]ΝΠΕΝ̣[- - - - - - - - - - - - - - - - - -]
[- - - - - -]*v* ἐὰν δ[ὲ - - - - - - - - - - - - - - - - -]
[- - - - - -]Α̣ΝΔ̣Ρ[- - - - - - - - - - - - - - - - - -]
[- -]

d

[- -]
[- - - - - - - . .]ΙΝ[- - - - - - - - - - - - - - - - - -]
[- - - - - -]ΩΕΠ̣[- - - - - - - - - - - - - - - - - -]
[- - - - - -]ΣΤΟ[- - - - - - - - - - - - - - - - - - -]
[- - - - - -]ΨΗΦ[- - - - - - - - - - - - - - - - - -]
[- - - - - -]ΗΙΘ[- - - - - - - - - - - - - - - - - - -]
[- - - - - - - .]Υ[- - - - - - - - - - - - - - - - - - - -]
[- -]

Fragment *b*, line 2: The base of the right diagonal of lambda survives.

Line 3: The top of a central vertical, probably an iota, is visible on the break.

Line 6: The stone breaks on the upper left corner of rho, without enough being preserved to rule out gamma, epsilon, or pi.

Fragment *c*, line 2: The base of the left hasta of the second nu is preserved on the break.

Line 3: There is no trace of a letter before the epsilon, though almost the entire stoichos is preserved.

Line 4: Both diagonals of alpha survive, but not its crossbar; likewise, both diagonals of delta are preserved, but not its base.

Fragment *d*, line 1: The lower two-thirds of these letters survive.

Line 2: The left vertical and part of the horizontal of pi are preserved.

Line 4: The left half of the loop of phi survives; the vertical is visible in the break.

Line 2: This may be the end of an imperative such as [ὀφειλέτ]ω or [ἐξέστ]ω.

Line 3: [ἐ]ς το[- - -]?

Line 4: Possibly some form of the word ψήφισμα, and thus, perhaps, part of a publication formula; more likely it is some part of the verb ψηφίζειν.

Line 5: Possibly the end of a verb such as [λυθ]ῆι or [ἀποκτείν]ηι, or a feminine dative, such as [τέχν]ηι.

If these fragments do derive from *Agora* XVI, no. 47, they should be designated fragments *r, s, t,* and *u* of the composite document.

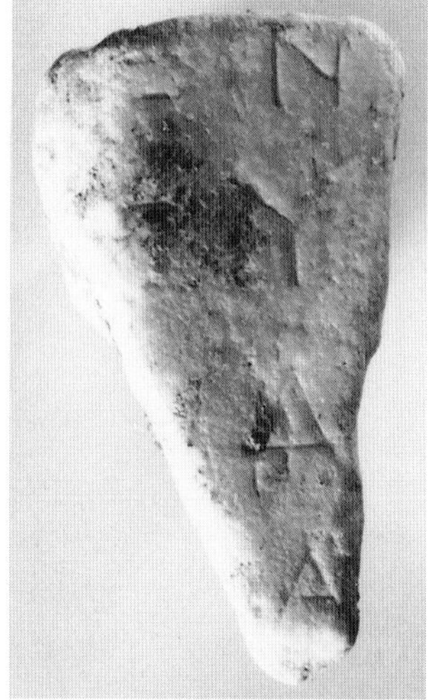

a

b

c

d

Figure 5. Fragments of the agreement between Athens and Stymphalos in Arkadia? (5): (a) fr. *a,* I 6384; (b) fr. *b,* I 4510a; (c) fr. *c,* I 4510b; (d) fr. *d,* I 2925

Figure 6. Fragment of a decree (possibly a proxeny decree) (6)

6 Fragment of a decree (possibly a proxeny decree) Fig. 6

I 3510. The upper right corner of a pedimental stele of Pentelic marble, brought in during February, 1936, from the area of the Stoa of Attalos (P–R 7–13). The smooth-dressed right side and part of the rough-picked back are preserved, with part of a crowning molding surviving above the inscribed face; part of the corner akroterion and the top of the raking cornice are preserved.

H. 0.48 (pediment, 0.07), W. 0.13, Th. 0.185 (face 0.165); L.H. 0.014 (line 1), 0.012 (lines 2–4), 0.011 (line 5); non-stoich.; vertical spacing between lines 1, 2, and 3 is 0.014; between lines 3, 4, 5, and 6 it is 0.012.

Before the mid-4th century B.C. Non-stoich.

[ἐπὶ - - - - - - - - - -] ἄρχοντος
[- - - - - - - - - - - .]ΕΡΑΚΩΙ κα̣[ὶ]
[- - - - - - - - - - - - . .]Δ̣ΑΜ[.]Ι̣
[- - - - - - - - - - - - . .]ΡΕΥΣ̣Ι̣[.]
[- - - - - - - - - - - - . . .]ΑΙΩΝ̣[. .]
[- - - - - - - - - - - - . . .]ΤΕ̣Υ̣[. . .]
[- - - - - - - - - - - - - - - - - - - -]

Line 2: The upper horizontal, part of the vertical, and the middle horizontal of epsilon survive; omega is followed by the top of a vertical, most likely iota; the base of the vertical and the tips of the diagonals of kappa are visible, followed by the diagonals and the right half of the horizontal of alpha.

Line 3: The apex of a triangular letter is visible before the alpha, probably a delta or a lambda.

Line 4: The upsilon is complete, though faint. After this, the lowest diagonal of a sigma is preserved, followed by the top of a vertical.

Line 5: The upper left corner of nu survives.

Line 6: The right half of the horizontal and the top of the vertical of tau, the upper left corner of epsilon, and the diagonals of upsilon are preserved.

The character of the letters is suited to the second quarter of the 4th century B.C.

Line 1: Spatial considerations lead me to suggest that the name of the archon of 365/4 B.C. should be restored here. Thus, [ἐπὶ Χίωνος] ἄρχοντος?[8]

Lines 2–3: [προξενία - -]εράκωι κα̣[ὶ - - -]δ̣άμ[ω]ι̣?[9]

Line 4: Perhaps [Μεγα]ρεῦσ̣ι̣, or [Γαργα]ρεῦσ̣ι̣?

Line 6: [- - ἐγραμμά]τε̣υ̣[εν]?

8. The secretary in 365/4 B.C. is now thought to have been Kephisios son of Epikrates Ionides (see *IG* II^2 216 + 261 and 217 = *SEG* XIV 47), but it is not yet proven that the system of appointing secretaries annually, rather than month-by-month, had been put into operation by 365/4 B.C.; the first occasion upon which an annual secretary definitely appears is 363/2 B.C. (*IG* II^2 109, 110, 111, etc.). See also Henry 2002, p. 92 and n. 5, for evidence that at least two secretaries served during 366/5 B.C. Thus, even if the year is 365/4 B.C., it is not possible to restore the secretary's name in line 6.

9. Cf. *IG* II^2 161, honoring two citizens of Megalopolis; *IG* II^2 162, honoring two citizens of Katania; and *IG* II^2 231 (+ EM 12823: see Lambert 2001b), honoring three men, probably citizens of Megara.

7 Fragment from the conclusion of a decree, and part of a law concerning the Mysteries of the Eleusinian Goddesses — Fig. 7

I 6868. A fragment of a stele of pale, bluish-gray Hymettian marble discovered on April 23, 1959, in the area of the Eleusinion (U 21), in a house wall. The rough-picked back is partly preserved. The face is badly abraded, but it is apparent that there is a vertical uninscribed space of 0.014 below line 7, indicating that a new document may begin in the next line.

H. 0.268, W. 0.157, Th. 0.088; L.H. 0.006–0.007; non-stoich. vert. 0.011.

Before the mid-4th century B.C. — Non-stoich.

[- -]
[- - - - . . . ca. 9 . . .]ΜΕ[- -]
[- - - - . . . ca. 9 . . .]ΠΙΣΤ[- - - - - - - - - - - - - - - - - - - -]
[- - - - . . . ca. 8 . .]Δ̣ΗΜΟΥ[- - - - - - - - - - - - - - - - - - - -]
[- - - - . . . ca. 8 . .]Ε̣ΡΟΥΕΘ̣Υ̣Σ̣[- - - - - - - - - - - - - - - - -]
[- - - - . . . ca. 8 . .] β̣ασιλεὺ[ς - - - - - - - - - - - - - - - - - -]
[- - - - . . . ca. 8 . .] ἐπιμελητὰ[ς - - - - - - - - - - - - - - - - -]
[- - - - . . ca. 7 . .]Ο̣ γραμμ̣α̣τεὺς ἐς [στήλην λιθίνην? - - -]
[- - - - . . ca. 7 . .] *vacat* 0.014 [- - - - - - - - - - - - - - - -]
[- - - - ca. 2] οἱ νομ̣όθετ[αι ο]ἱ ἐπὶ Θ̣[- - - - - - - - - - - - - - -]
[- - - - ca. 2]Ο̣Σ̣[. . κα]τὰ τὸν ν̣όμ[ο]ν [- - - - - - - - - - - - - -]
[- - - - . . . . . . ca. 15 . . . . . .]ΟΘΕ[- - - - - - - - - - - - - - - - -]
[- - - - τὸ]ν γρα[μμ]ατ[έα] το[ῦ δήμου - - - - - - - - - - - -]
[- - - - . . ca. 6 . ἐ]πιμελη[τὰς - - - - - - - - - - - - - - - - - -]
[- - - - . . ca. 8 . .]ΣΘΕΤ[- -]
[- - - - . . . ca. 9 . . .]ΝΥ[- -]
[- - - - . . . ca. 9 . . .]Η[- -]
[- - - - . . . ca. 9 . . .]ΑΤ[- -]
[- - - - . . . ca. 8 . .]ΙΟΣΟ[- -]
[- - - - . . . ca. 9 . . .]ΝΑ[- -]
[- - - - . . . ca. 9 . . .]ΕΞ[- -]
[- - - - . . . . ca. 11 . . . .]Ο[- -]
[- -]

Line 3: The base of a right diagonal survives at left.

Line 4: The right half of a bottom horizontal survives at the left, more likely that of an epsilon than of a delta; at the right edge the outline of a circular letter is followed by the base of a central vertical and then by a flattish diagonal, probably the lowest diagonal of a sigma.

Line 5: The upper loop and part of the vertical of beta survive

Line 7: The upper curve of a circular letter is preserved at the left edge; in the sixth and seventh stoichoi the left apex of the second mu and the apex of alpha survive.

Line 8: There is no trace of any lettering on the stone and, in any case, the vertical space is too great for a single line alone; I presume that this space divided the end of one text from the beginning of another.

Line 9: At left the first four letters are reasonably clear; after these the right apex of mu survives. The next four letters are clear, but then the surface is pitted

Figure 7. Fragment from the conclusion of a decree, and part of a law concerning the Mysteries of the Eleusinian Goddesses (7)

and three letters have disappeared. The next four letters are clear, but at the right only the outline of a circular letter is visible.

Lines 11–21: The lettering is increasingly worn and indistinct.

Whether or not an archon formula appears in line 9, the character of the script suggests a date close to that of *Agora* XVI, no. 56, and the context may be the same.[10]

Line 2: [ἐ]πιστ[άτας], or [ἐ]πιστ[άταις]? Cf. *Agora* XVI, no. 56A, line 48, and no. 56B, line 8, respectively.

Line 3: [τοῦ] δήμου [τοῦ Ἀθηναίων]?

Line 9: Surely this is an archon formula: ἐπὶ Θ[εέλλου ἄρχοντος? (351/50 B.C.)

10. See Clinton 1980; he lists in his n. 9 several other Agora fragments that, at one time, were considered as possible candidates for this stele, and the document here discussed is one of these. Clinton's list includes also two other fragments published here: I 6065 (= **90**, below), and I 6582 (= **47**, below).

8 Fragments from the conclusion of a decree — Fig. 8

I 5823, I 6487. Two fragments of a stele of heavily weathered Pentelic marble discovered at different times and in different places. There is no join, but fragment *a* probably lies above and to the left of fragment *b*, so that its line 4 corresponds to line 1 of fragment *b*.

Fragment *a* (I 5823) was discovered on May 13, 1939, east of the Post-Herulian Wall, in the west porch of the Library of Pantainos (R 14), in a pillaged wall trench. It is broken all around and on the back.

H. 0.115, W. 0.078, Th. 0.018.

Fragment *b* (I 6487) was discovered on March 29, 1952, on Areopagus Street, east of the Church of the Holy Apostles (Q 15), in Ottoman fill. It is broken all around and on the back.

H. 0.145, W. 0.16, Th. 0.085.

Both fragments: L.H. 0.010–0.012; stoich. 0.02 (square).

Before the mid-4th century B.C. — Stoich. 29

a
[- -]
[. . 5 . .]AΜ̣[. . . . . 22 . . . .]
[. . 5 . .]ΠΛΗ̣[. . . . . 21 . . . .]
[. . 5 . .]Α̣ΔΕ̣[. . . . . 21 . . . .]
[. . ἀνα]γρά[ψαι δὲ τόδε τὸ ψ]ή̣[φίσμα τὸν] *b*
[γραμμ]α̣τέ̣[α τῆς βολῆς] ⟦εἰ⟧ς στ[ήλην λιθ]-
[ίνην κα]ὶ̣ [θε͂ναι ἐν ἀκ]ρ̣οπόλε̣[ι· εἰς δὲ τ]-
[ὴν ἀναγραφὴν τῆς στήλ]ης δο͂[ναι τὸν τ]-
[αμίαν το͂ δήμο ΔΔ δραχ]μὰς ἐ[κ τῶν κατὰ]
[ψηφίσματ᾽ ἀναλισκομέ]νων̣ [τῶι δήμωι]
vacat

Line 1: The steep first diagonal of mu survives above the lambda of line 2.

Line 2: The right vertical and part of the horizontal of pi, a complete lambda, and the base of the first vertical of eta survive.

Line 3: The right diagonal of an alpha or lambda survives, but the weathering of the stone is such that it is not possible to say whether there was a horizontal stroke, as of an alpha. The horizontal of the delta is very faint, compared with its diagonals; the vertical and traces of the horizontals of epsilon are visible.

Line 4: The top and bottom of the left vertical of eta are preserved on fragment *b*, in the break above the tau of line 5.

Line 5: On fragment *a*, the base of the right diagonal of alpha and the upper left corner of epsilon survive; on fragment *b*, the tip of the lowest diagonal of sigma is preserved above the first omicron of line 6; to the left of this, the horizontals of epsilon are very faint and the iota is inscribed off-center, as if epsilon was first omitted and the mistake later corrected.

Line 6: On fragment *a*, the top of the iota may survive, below the tau of line 5. On fragment *b*, the loop of rho and the upper left corner of epsilon are preserved.

Line 8: The left and right apices of mu are visible in the first stoichos; the lower left corner of epsilon survives in the fourth.

Line 9: The top of a vertical stroke survives in the abrasion, surely the left hasta of a nu.

The use of E for EI and of O for OY, as restored here, probably indicates that the date of this document is not later than the 350s B.C.[11]

11. See Threatte 1980, pp. 299–323, 349–352.

a

b

Figure 8. Fragments from the conclusion of a decree (8): (a) fr. *a*, I 5823; (b) fr. *b*, I 6487

9 Fragment of a decree Fig. 9

I 3666. The upper left corner of a stele of Pentelic marble discovered on March 3, 1936, north of the Civic Offices (I 11), in a mixed Byzantine and Ottoman context. The flat, rough-picked top, pick-dressed left side and, perhaps, back are preserved. The top has a drafted edge 0.01 wide along the front; the back, if original, is smooth-dressed: the thickness, however, suggests that the back has been reworked in later times. On the front, the left margin of 0.016 is unusually wide.

H. 0.057, W. 0.091, Th. 0.048; L.H. 0.007–0.008; stoich. 0.014 (square, lines 2–3).

Before the mid-4th century B.C. Stoich.

Θ ε ο [ί *vacat*]
ΔΕΙΝ[- - - - - - - - - - - - - - -]
Δ[- - - - - - - - - - - - - - - - - -]
[- - - - - - - - - - - - - - - - - - -]

Figure 9. Fragment of a decree (9)

Line 1: The upper half of omicron is preserved; theta and epsilon are placed above the first and third letters of line 2.

Line 3: The apex of a triangular letter is preserved, along with the left part of a curved horizontal at the base of the same stoichos, similar to that of the delta of line 2.

The character of the letters is suited to the second quarter of the 4th century B.C.

Lines 2–3: The wide margin suggests that this is an honorific title or a secretary formula, and thus part of a decree of the State. Several names suggest themselves for the period in question.[12]

10 Fragment from the conclusion of a decree Fig. 10

I 5521. A fragment of a stele of Pentelic marble discovered on June 8, 1938, below Klepsydra (T 26), at the east end of south wall B of the paved court. It is broken all around and on the back.

H. 0.132, W. 0.072, Th. 0.095; L.H. 0.007–0.008 (lines 1–4), 0.008–0.009 (lines 5–6); stoich. 0.014 (square, lines 1–4), hor. 0.014, vert. 0.015 (lines 4–6).

Before the mid-4th century B.C. Stoich. 37

[- -]
[. . . . . .13. . . . . .]K[. . . . . .23. . . . .]
[. . . . ἀναγράψα]ι δ[ὲ τόδε τὸ ψήφισμα τὸν γραμμα]-
[τέα τῆς βουλῆ]ς ἐν [στήληι λιθίνηι καὶ στῆσαι ἐ]-
[ν ἀκροπόλει· εἰ]ς δ̣ὲ [τὴν πόησιν καὶ τὴν ἀναγράφ]-
[ην τῆς στήλης δ]ο̣ῦ[ναι τὸν ταμίαν τοῦ δήμου πεν]-
[τήκοντα δραχμ]ὰς [ἐκ τῶν εἰς τὰ κατὰ ψηφίσματα]
[*vacat?*] *vacat*

Line 4: The right third of the stoichos before sigma is uninscribed; thus the missing letter was an iota; at the right edge the upper part of the vertical of epsilon survives in the break.

Lines 5 and 6: These lines appear to have been engraved by a different, less skilled hand, with slightly larger lettering.

The character of the letters is suited to the second quarter of the 4th century B.C.

Lines 6–7: There is insufficient room for a reference to the *analiskomena* fund. For such an omission, cf. *IG* II^2 140, lines 35–38, which seems to be of much the same date.

Figure 10. Fragment from the conclusion of a decree (10)

11 Fragment of a decree Fig. 11

I 970. Fragment of a stele of Pentelic marble discovered on June 15, 1933, east of the Propylon of the New Bouleuterion (I 11), in a late wall. The smooth-dressed top is preserved.

H. 0.022, W. 0.11, Th. 0.059; L.H. 0.007–0.008; semi-stoich. hor. ca. 0.01, horizontal spacing 0.004–0.005.

336/5 B.C. Semi-stoich.

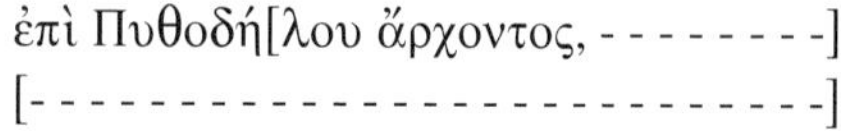

ἐπὶ Πυθοδή[λου ἄρχοντος, - - - - - - - -]
[- -]

12. See *LGPN* II, pp. 100–102.

Figure 11. Fragment of a decree (**11**)

Line 1: The iota is placed inter-stoichos; otherwise the spacing is fairly regular. The bottom of the first vertical and part of the horizontal of eta survive; thus the name and date of the archon are assured. The photograph is misleading: there is no trace on the stone of what appears to be an omicron below the upsilon.

12 Fragment from the conclusion of an honorific decree Fig. 12

I 4265. A fragment of a block of black Eleusinian limestone discovered on June 14, 1936, in the southwestern corner of the north room of the Annex to the Stoa of Zeus (G 6), in packing below the level of the marble slabs. It is broken all around and on the back, and has been mended from two fragments that were found together. Faint horizontal, as well as some vertical, scribed guidelines are visible.

H. 0.082, W. 0.112, Th. 0.076; L.H. 0.005; stoich. hor. 0.0093, vert. 0.0095.

Ca. 350–335 B.C.? Stoich.

[- -]
[- - - - - - . .]Σ̣[- -]
[- - - - - - . .] ἐ̣ν τῶι δ[ήμωι - - - - - - - - - - - - - - - - - - -]
[- - - - - - . .]AI τῶι δήμω[ι -]
[- - - - - - . .]Ο̣ΜΟΝ χρυσῶι σ̣[τεφάνωι - - - - - - - - - - -]
[- - - - - - τῶ]ι δήμωι· ἀναγρά[ψαι δὲ - - - - - - - - - - - -]
[- - - - - - . . .]Θ̣ΕΙΣΘΑΙΤΟΑΝΑ[- - - - - - - - - - - - - - - - -]
vacat

Line 1: The lowest diagonal of a sigma survives above the epsilon of line 2.

Line 4: In the first stoichos the right half of a circular letter survives, either omicron or theta.

Line 6: The lower right part of a circular letter survives in the first stoichos.

Figure 12. Fragment from the conclusion of an honorific decree (**12**)

Line 4: [- -]ọμον (or [- -]θ̣μον): the end of a personal name in the accusative?

Line 6: τὸ ἀνά[θημα]? Cf. *IG* II^2 223B, line 16. If this restoration is correct, this fragment is likely to derive from a statue base similar to *IG* II^2 223, three honorific decrees dated to 343/2 B.C., also inscribed upon black Eleusinian limestone, which may have been the model for this document, or vice versa.[13]

13 Fragment of a decree Fig. 13

I 5501. A fragment of a stele of Pentelic marble discovered on June 3, 1938, in the Klepsydra antechamber (T 27:1), in a Classical context. It is broken all around and on the back. The face seems to have been polished.

H. 0.068, W. 0.051, Th. 0.072; L.H. 0.007; stoich. 0.0135 (square).

Ca. 350–335 B.C.? Stoich. 38

[- -]
[. . . . 10 . . . .]ΠΛ̣[. . . . . 26 . . . .]
[. . . . 10 . . . .]ΝΤΟ[. . . . . 25 . . . .]
[. . . . 10 . . . .] ἀγαθ[ῆι τύχηι δεδόχθαι τῆι βουλῆι]
[τοὺς προέδρο]υς ο[ἳ ἂν λάχωσιν προεδρεύειν κτλ.]
[- -]

Line 1: The right half of the horizontal and the second vertical of pi are preserved, though damaged; to the right of the pi the lower part of a left diagonal survives, with no trace of a crossbar or base.

The date offered here is based upon the characteristics of the lettering.

Figure 13. Fragment of a decree (13)

14 Fragment of an honorific decree for Phyleus of Oinoe Fig. 14

I 5280. A fragment of a stele of Pentelic marble discovered on March 3, 1938, on the line of the west stair-parapet of the north slope of the Acropolis (T 23), in a late context. It is broken all around and on the back. It is part of *IG* II^2 330 + 445 (EM 7136 + 7218), given below, starting at line 5, and may join the right edge of lines 7–14 of EM 7136.[14]

H. 0.126, W. 0.06, Th. 0.049; L.H. 0.004–0.005; stoich. hor. 0.009, vert. 0.0095 (lines 1–3), 0.008 (lines 4–6), 0.0085 (lines 7–8).

335/4 B.C. Stoich. 46

[ἐπ]-
[ε]ιδὴ Φυλεὺς χειροτ[ονηθεὶς . . . . 21 . . . . κα]-
[ὶ] τῶι δήμωι ἐπὶ Πυθο[δή]λο[υ ἄρχοντος τὴν ἀρχήν, ἐφ' ἣν ἐχειρ]-
[οτ]ονήθη, ἦρχεν καλ[ῶς κ]αὶ κ[ατὰ τοὺς νόμους καὶ ὑπὸ τῶν πρυ]-
[τα]νειῶν πασῶν ἐστ[εφ]ανώ[θη χρυσῶι στεφάνωι . . . . 10 . . . .]
[. . . . τῆς β]ουλῆς [κα]ὶ̣ τῆς ΕΚ̣[. . . . . 25 . . . .]
[. .]Μ[. . . 7 . . .]Γ[. . . .]Ο̣ΔΗΜΟ̣Σ[. . . . . 19 . . . . κατὰ τὸ]-
[ν ν]όμον, κα[. . . 6 . . .]ΡΙΤΟΓΕ̣[. . . . . 26 . . . .]
[. .] τῶι δήμωι, ἐ[παιν]έ̣σαι τ[ὸν . . . . 18 . . . . καὶ τοῦ]
[δή]μου τὸν ἐπὶ [Πυθο]δ̣ήλο[υ ἄρχοντος Φυλέα Παυσανίου Οἰνα]-
[ῖο]ν κτλ.

The text of the new fragment is underlined.

Line 10 (= line 4 of I 5280): The base of iota and the top of the vertical of kappa survive.

13. See Walbank 2002, p. 62, no. 3.

14. Stephen Tracy (*ADT*, p. 119) identified this fragment as the work of the "Cutter of *IG* II^2 330 + 445." It has not been possible to take the Agora fragment to the Epigraphic Museum, and in any case, since *IG* II^2 330 is now set in plaster, its edge cannot be examined.

Figure 14. Fragment of an honorific decree for Phyleus of Oinoe (14)

Line 12 (= line 6 of I 5280): The top of the loop of a rho survives to left of iota; at right, after gamma, a left vertical survives, with part of an abraded horizontal at its base.

Line 13 (= line 7 of I 5280): The vertical and the top horizontal of epsilon are preserved.

Line 14 (= line 8 of I 5280): The apex of delta survives.

Line 6: [ἱεροποιεῖν τῆι τε βουλῆι] *IG* II^2 330; [γραμματεὺς τῆι τε βουλῆι] Matthaiou.[15]

Lines 9–10: [καὶ ἐπηινέθ|η ὑπὸ τῆς β]ουλῆς [καὶ τοῦ δήμου] *IG* II^2 330; instead of [καὶ τοῦ δήμου], perhaps [κα]ὶ τῆς ἐκ̣[κλησίας]?

Line 11: In the original publication, as reported and confirmed by Ulrich Koehler in *IG* II 5 128b, a mu was also read in the third stoichos, and the gamma surviving in the eleventh stoichos was printed as the upper left corner of a letter such as gamma or epsilon. Stephen Lambert informs me *(per ep.)* that slight traces of the mu in the third stoichos are visible on the stone and are confirmed by a squeeze; readings other than gamma in the eleventh stoichos are not excluded. He suggests that the letters ΟΔΗΜΟΣ may be part of a name.

Lines 12–13: [δεδόχθαι] τῶι δήμωι *IG* II^2 330; [τὸν ἱεροποιὸν τῆς βουλῆς] *IG* II^2 330; [τὸν γραμματέα τῆς βουλῆς] Matthaiou.

15. Angelos Matthaiou *apud* Lambert 2004, pp. 89 and 92–96, no. 3; photograph of *IG* II^2 330 + 445: Lambert 2004, fig. 5:3.

15 Fragment of a law concerning religious reforms — Fig. 15

I 4664. A fragment of a stele of pale gray Hymettian marble discovered on March 30, 1937, on the north slope of the Acropolis, east of the

Figure 15. Fragment of a law concerning religious reforms (**15**)

Post-Herulian Wall (V 23), in a late context. It is broken all around and on the back.

H. 0.076, W. 0.094, Th. 0.08; L.H. 0.004–0.005; stoich. 0.0095 (square).

335/4 B.C. Stoich.

[- -]

[- - - - - - - - - - - ἀ]λ̣λ' ἐὰ⟦ν⟧ μὴ̣ [- - - - - - - - - - -]

[- - - - - - - - - - - .]HI ἐκ τῆς Δ[- - - - - - - - - - - - -]

[- - - - - - - - - - -]ΑΙΕΡΟΣΥΛΙ[- - - - - - - - - - - - - -]

[- - - - - - - - - - -]Ι ὁ δῆμος Ψ⟦Η⟧[- - - - - - - - - - - -]

[- - - - - - - - - - - .]ΙΣ τῆι ΠΡΟ̣[- - - - - - - - - - - - - -]

[- - - - - - - - - - - .]Ν τὸν κόσμ̣[ον - - - - - - - - - - - -]

[- - - - - - - - - - - .]Ι τὸν κὀ̣[σμον - - - - - - - - - - - - -]

[- - - - - - - - - - - . .]Β̣Α̣Σ[- - - - - - - - - - - - - - - - - -]

[- -]

Line 1: The lower half of the right diagonal of the first lambda is preserved. In the fifth stoichos the mason first inscribed iota, then corrected this to nu. After nu the lower half of mu survives, followed by a well-preserved left vertical; the stoichos is abraded in such a way that either eta or epsilon could be read here.

Line 3: The bottom of the right diagonal and part of the horizontal of alpha survive.

Line 4: In the ninth stoichos the mason first inscribed iota, then corrected this to eta.

Line 5: After rho, a circular depression seems to be the remains of an omicron or, perhaps, an omega.

Line 6: The lower part of the left diagonal of mu survives.

Line 7: The upper left quadrant of omicron is preserved.

Line 8: The upper half of the top loop of beta survives, followed by the apex of alpha and the upper two diagonals of sigma.

The marble, patterns of cleavage, lettering, and spacing are identical with those of *IG* II² 333 (EM 7077 + 7147–7151), and I believe that this is yet another fragment of that document, but there is no join with any of the fragments so far identified.[16]

Line 1: Or μὲ̣[ν - -]?
Line 2: ἕκτης is less likely.
Line 3: ἱ̣εροσυλί[α]?
Line 4: [ὅτ]ι ὁ δῆμος ψ⟦η⟧[φιεῖται]?
Line 7: [ἐπ]ὶ τὸν κό[σμον]? Cf. *IG* II² 333, fragments *c–f*, lines 22–23.
Line 8: A reference to the Archon Basileus?

16 Fragment of a decree Fig. 16

I 5500. A fragment of a stele of Pentelic marble discovered on June 2, 1938, in the Klepsydra antechamber (T 27:1), in a Classical context. It is broken all around and on the back. The face is polished.

H. 0.095, W. 0.042, Th. 0.006; L.H. 0.007–0.008; stoich. 0.0165 (square).

Ca. 337–324 B.C. Stoich.

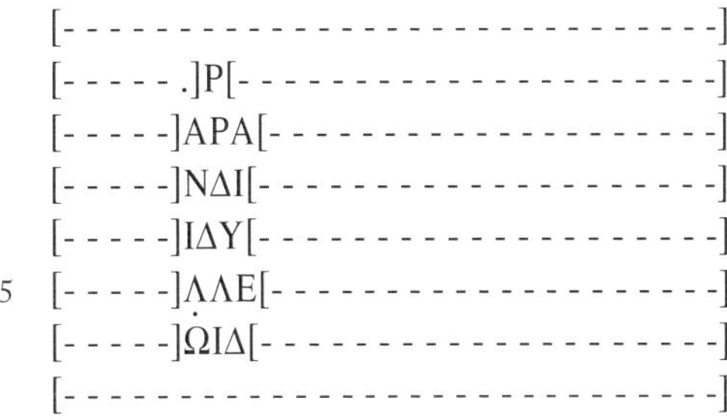

[- -]
[- - - - - .]Ρ[- -]
[- - - - -]ΑΡΑ[- - - - - - - - - - - - - - - - - - -]
[- - - - -]ΝΔΙ[- - - - - - - - - - - - - - - - - - -]
[- - - - -]ΙΔΥ[- - - - - - - - - - - - - - - - - - -]
[- - - - -]ΛΛΕ[- - - - - - - - - - - - - - - - - - -]
[- - - - -]Ω̣ΙΔ[- - - - - - - - - - - - - - - - - - -]
[- -]

Figure 16. Fragment of a decree (16)

Line 1: The base of the vertical and the beginning of the lower curve of the loop of rho survive.

Line 4: The stone breaks on the right side of the vertical of iota.

Line 5: The base of a right diagonal survives in the first stoichos.

Line 6: The upper right part of omega and a trace of its right horizontal extender survive within an abrasion. Tracy attributes this to the "Cutter of *IG* II² 354," active between 337 and 324 B.C.[17]

Line 2: [Μ]αρα[θώνιος]?
Line 3: [- -]ν Δι[ομειεύς]?
Line 4: [ἔδοξενǀ τῶι δήμω]ι· Δυ[- - - - - εἶπεν]?
Line 5: [ἀπαγγέ]λ̣λε[ι - -]?

This may be the beginning of a decree in which a list of *symproedroi* appears before the resolution and orator formulas.[18]

16. The most recent edition of this document is Schwenk 1985, pp. 108–126, no. 21. Schwenk reports (p. 108) that another fragment in the Epigraphic Museum (*g* = EM 2459) will be published by C. Peppas-Delmousou, and that it joins fragment *d*. The fragments have been reedited by Lambert (2005, p. 135, no. 6; pp. 137–143, figs. 5–7), of whose comments I have made use here.

17. *ADT*, pp. 104–111; description of lettering, pp. 104–105; photograph, p. 105, fig. 5.

18. For such boards, see Dow 1963, esp. p. 335.

Figure 17. Fragment of an honorific decree? (**17**)

17 Fragment of an honorific decree? Fig. 17

I 3063. A fragment of a stele of Pentelic marble discovered on September 30, 1935, between the Stoa of Attalos and the north end of the Odeion (O 9), in a modern house wall. The pick-dressed left side is preserved, with a margin of 0.018. Almost vertical marks of the finishing rasp are visible, running from top left to bottom right.

H. 0.171, W. 0.155, Th. 0.108; L.H. 0.01–0.011; stoich. 0.02 (square).

Ca. 337–324 B.C.? Stoich.

[- -]
[. . .]ỊTỊ[- - - - - - - - - - - - - - - -]
[. .]MENO[- - - - - - - - - - - - - -]
[. .]EIΠ[- - - - - - - - - - - - - - - -]
[.]ΣAN[- - - - - - - - - - - - - - - -]
ẠIHI[- - - - - - - - - - - - - - - - - -]
ṆTI[- - - - - - - - - - - - - - - - - - -]
AN[- - - - - - - - - - - - - - - - - - -]
Ọ[- - - - - - - - - - - - - - - - - - - -]
[- -]

Line 1: The bases of two verticals survive in the first and third stoichoi, the first slightly right of center; iotas on this stone tend to be placed off-center to the right, as in line 3; the other vertical is central, like the second iota of line 5; since there is no trace of the tip of a horizontal, tau is ruled out, despite the impression given by the photograph.

Line 3: Parts of all three letter strokes of pi are visible in the abrasion.

Line 5: The base of a right diagonal survives.

Line 8: The top of the upper loop of a circular letter is preserved below the alpha of line 7.

The shapes of alpha, epsilon, eta, nu, and pi, and the tendency to thicken the free ends of straight strokes, are surely the work of the "Cutter of *IG* II² 354," active between 337 and 324 B.C.[19]

Lines 1–3: The names of a board of *symproedroi,* without patronymics and probably with abbreviated demotics?[20]

Line 3: εἶπ[εν]?

Lines 5–6: [ἐν πα]|ντὶ [καιρῶι]?

18 Fragment from the conclusion of a decree — Fig. 18

I 4955. A fragment of a stele of Pentelic marble discovered on June 8, 1937, on the north slope of the Acropolis (U–V 24–25), on the surface. The pick-dressed right side is preserved, with a drafted edge 0.01 wide; the right margin is 0.014.

H. 0.07, W. 0.06, Th. 0.025; L.H. 0.0055; stoich. 0.011 (square).

Figure 18. Fragment from the conclusion of a decree (18)

Ca. 337–323 B.C.? — Stoich. 59

[ἀναγράψα]-
[ι δὲ τόδε τὸ ψήφισμα τὸν γραμματέα τὸν κατὰ πρυτανείαν ἐν στήληι λιθίν]η-
[ι καὶ στῆσαι ἐν ἀκροπόλει· εἰς δὲ τὴν ἀναγράφην τῆς στήλης δοῦναι τὸν τ]αμ-
[ίαν τοῦ δήμου . . . δραχμὰς ἐκ τῶν κατὰ ψηφίσματα ἀναλισκομένων τῶι] δ̣ήμω-
[ι. *vacat*?] *vacat*

Line 3: The lower part of the right diagonal of delta survives.

I believe that the few surviving letters are characteristic of the work of the "Cutter of *IG* II² 337," active between 337 and 323 B.C.;[21] note the wide eta, awkwardly shaped mu, and omega set high in the middle of the letter space.

The very wide margin suggests that the stele from which this fragment derives was both tall and very wide. This may well be part of an ephebic text of the 4th century B.C.

19 Fragment from the conclusion of an honorific decree — Fig. 19

I 3023. A fragment of a stele of Pentelic marble discovered on May 29, 1935, inside the base in the east side of the south part of the Metroön (I 10), in a disturbed context. It is broken all around and on the back.

H. 0.085, W. 0.075, Th. 0.042; L.H. 0.006–0.007; stoich. 0.015 (square).

Ca. 340–320 B.C. — Stoich.

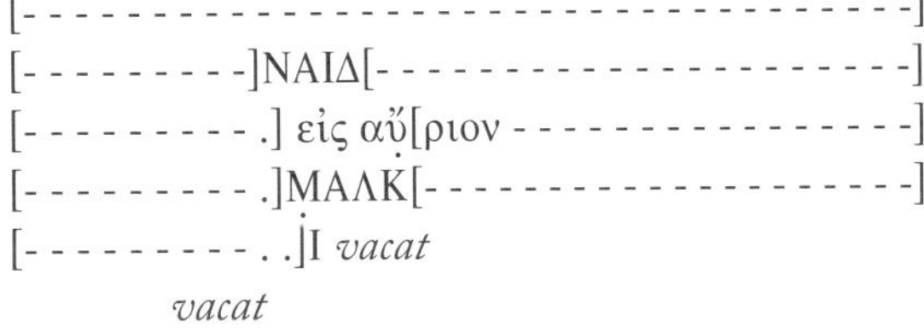

[- -]
[- - - - - - - - -]ΝΑΙΔ[- -]
[- - - - - - - - - .] εἰς αὐ̣[ριον - - - - - - - - - - - - - - - - -]
[- - - - - - - - - .]Μ̣ΑΛΚ[- - - - - - - - - - - - - - - - - - - -]
[- - - - - - - - - . .]Ι *vacat*
vacat

Line 2: The bottom of the vertical of upsilon is preserved.

Line 3: Before the alpha the apex of a triangular letter survives; its position and steepness suggest that it is the second apex of a mu.

Tracy attributes this fragment to the "Cutter of *IG* II² 244," active between 340/39 and ca. 320 B.C.[22]

19. See n. 17, above.

20. See n. 18, above.

21. *ADT,* pp. 112–116; description of lettering, pp. 112–114; photograph, p. 113, fig. 7.

22. *ADT,* pp. 96–103; description of lettering, pp. 96–97; photograph, p. 97, fig. 3.

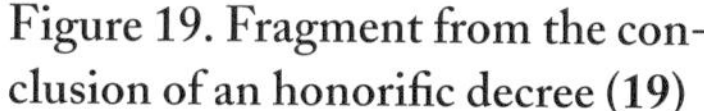
Figure 19. Fragment from the conclusion of an honorific decree (19)

Lines 1–2: [καλέσαι - - - ἐπὶ ξένια(?) εἰς τὸ πρυτανεῖον] εἰς αὔ̣[ριον].

Lines 3–4: [τέλεσι τοῖς] Μ̣αλκ[- - - ἐν στήληι λιθίνηι καὶ στῆσαι ἐν Ἀκροπόλε]ι?

20 Fragment of a decree — Fig. 20

I 5642. A fragment of a stele of micaceous Pentelic marble discovered between February 6 and 11, 1939, in the industrial area southwest of the Market Square (A–E 16–23), in a modern context. It is broken all around and on the back.

H. 0.083, W. 0.073, Th. 0.06; L.H. 0.005–0.006; stoich. 0.014 (square).

Ca. 340–320 B.C.? — Stoich.

[- -]
[. . . .⁸. . . .]ΑΣ[- -]
[. . .⁶. . .]τ̣ει ἱ[σταμένου - - - - - - - - - - - - - - -]
[. . ⁵. . τῆ]ς πρ[υτανείας - - - - - - - - - - - - - -]
[τῶν προ]έ̣δρων̣ [ἐπεψήφιζεν - - - - - - - - - - -]
[. . . ⁷. . .]Χ̇[.]Ρ[- - - - - - - - - - - - - - - - - - - -]
[- -]

Figure 20. Fragment of a decree (20)

Line 1: In a strong oblique light the bases of the diagonals and the crossbar of alpha are visible above the first iota of line 2, followed by the lower diagonals of sigma.

Line 2: In the first stoichos the right tip of the horizontal of tau is preserved.

Line 4: The right tip of the upper horizontal of epsilon and the bottom of the first vertical of nu are preserved in the first and last stoichoi, respectively.

The baseline of delta slopes up to right and the left diagonal is slightly longer than the right; the middle horizontal of epsilon is shorter than the outer ones; pi is relatively short but wide; the vertical of rho curves a little at its top so that this letter

Figure 21. Fragment of a decree (**21**), detail

seems to be falling forward; the lowest diagonal of sigma extends down below the bottom of the stoichos and the upper diagonal is almost flat; chi is very small; and omega has a tall, oval loop with slightly drooping horizontal extenders. These features are characteristic of the style described by Tracy as "*Litterae Volgares Saec. IV*," that is, of the 330s and 320s B.C.[23]

Line 1: [. . .]άσ[ιος ἐγραμμάτευεν]? Possibly Aristonous son of Aristonous Anagyrasios, secretary in 332/1 B.C.
Line 5: [Ἀ]χ[α]ρ[νεύς]? or [Ἀ]χ[ε]ρ[δούσιος]?

21 Fragment of a decree — Fig. 21

I 2239. A fragment of a stele of micaceous Pentelic marble discovered on December 10, 1934, over the east end of the Middle Stoa (N 13), in a modern house wall. The stipple-dressed left side survives, slightly undercutting the face; the left margin is 0.009. The fragment is badly worn and discolored and has suffered fire damage.

H. 0.238, W. 0.141, Th. 0.104; L.H. 0.007; stoich. hor. 0.011, vert. 0.013.

Ca. 340–320 B.C.? — Stoich.

[- -]
[. . . .] ὅτι δο[κεῖ - - - - - - - - - -]
[. . . . .] δέχε[σθαι - - - - - - - - -]
[.]λ̣[. . .] γε̣γο[νέναι - - - - - - - -]
[.]ΟΛ̣[- - - - - - - - - - - - - - - - - -]
[.]ΤΟ̣[- - - - - - - - - - - - - - - - - -]
[.]Λ̣[- - - - - - - - - - - - - - - - - - -]
[- -]

Line 3: The faint outline of a triangular letter survives at left; despite heavy abrasion the right end of the topmost horizontal of epsilon survives between the two gammas, and after the second gamma the outline of omicron is visible, each letter set a little to the right of those of line 2.

Line 4: A circular letter and the apex of a triangular letter are visible where the surface is preserved at left; there are indecipherable traces of letters where the surface is preserved at right.

23. *ADT*, pp. 76–81; description of lettering, pp. 76–77.

Line 5: The upper half of a circular letter follows the tau.
Line 6: The apex of a triangular letter survives.

Lines 3–4: A clause in which a priest is praised for his report regarding sacrifices: [ἀπαγγ|έ]λ̣[λει] γε̣γο[νέναι ἐν τοῖς ἱεροῖς]? For examples of about the same date as this fragment, cf. *IG* II² 354 and 410; see also **16**, line 5.

22 Fragment of a decree concerning *epheboi* Fig. 22

I 794. A fragment of a stele of bluish Pentelic marble discovered on May 8, 1933, outside the southeast corner of the Stoa of Zeus (I 7), in a Late Roman context. The face and right lateral are preserved, with a left margin of 0.003. The face bears a carving of a laurel wreath, but no inscription.

H. 0.104, W. 0.109, Th. (= W. of right lateral) 0.046; L.H. 0.006; stoich. 0.0105 (square).

Ca. 335–320 B.C.? Stoich.

Face A — *Wreath*

Face B (right lateral)

[- -]
Ṭ̣ỊM[- -]
ΤΑΣΕ[- τῶι δήμ]-
ωι τῶ[ι Ἀθηναίων? - - - - - - - - - - - - - - - - - - ἐ̣]-
φ̣ηβο[- ἀνδρα]-
γα̣θί[ας - εἰς τ]-
ὸν δῆ[μον -]
ENTA[- -]
ΟΥΔ̣[- -]
AN[- -]
[- -]

Figure 22. Fragment of a decree concerning *epheboi* (**22**): face A *(left)*, and face B *(right)*

Line 1: The lower two-thirds of two central verticals survive in the first two stoichoi; the mu is very wide, its two outer strokes nearly vertical, its inner strokes forming a shallow vee, of which the base survives.

Line 5: Part of the left diagonal of alpha survives.

Line 8: The apex of a triangular letter survives in the third stoichos.

Line 9: The upper left corner of nu is preserved.

I believe the letter forms are characteristic of the late 330s or the 320s B.C.

Lines 1–2: [τοὺς ἐφήβους τοὺς ἐνγραφέν]|τας ἐ[πὶ - - - - - - ἄρχοντος]?

Lines 4–5: [ἀρετῆς ἕνεκα καὶ ἀνδρα]|γα̣θί[ας τῆς]?

Lines 6–7: [τοὺς ἐνγραφ]|έντα[ς], or [τοὺς χειροτονηθ]|έντα[ς]?

The presence of a wreath on the adjoining face of the stele and the mention of ephebes in lines 3–4 suggest that this is part of a large, multi-faced ephebic document, necessitating a line of ca. 35–45 letters or more. The *ephebia* seems to have been reorganized under Lykourgos in ca. 336/5 B.C., and ephebic decrees appear frequently after this date.[24]

23 Fragments of a decree perhaps concerning *epheboi*? Fig. 23

I 4902c, I 4902d. Two fragments of a stele of Pentelic marble discovered on June 16, 1937, on the north slope of the Acropolis (T 26–27), in the fill of the Post-Herulian Wall over the paved court below Klepsydra. On both fragments, the right side slightly undercuts the inscribed face and is smooth-dressed.

Fragment *a* (I 4902c). The right side is preserved; the margin is 0.016.

H. 0.173, W. 0.118, Th. 0.046.

Fragment *b* (I 4902d). The right side is preserved; the margin is 0.019. There is a vertical uninscribed space of 0.128 below the last line.

H. 0.174, W. 0.115, Th. 0.067.

Both fragments: L.H. 0.008–0.009; stoich. hor. 0.0185, vert. 0.0183.

Ca. 335–320 B.C.? Stoich.

a

[- -]
[- . . τῶν προέδρ][[ω]][ν]
[ἐπεψήφιζεν - - - - - - - - - - ἔδοξεν τηῖ βο]υλ-
[ῆι καὶ τωῖ δήμωι - - - - - - - - - . . . . 10 . . . .]ITH
[- . . . . 10 . . . .]OYA
[- . . . . 10 . . . .]ATH
[- . . . . 9 . . . .]Λ̣EIK
[- . . . . 9 . . . .]Α̣TON
[- . . . . 9 . . . .]IΠPA
[- . . . . 9 . . . .]AIΠE
[- -]

b

[- -]
[- . . . . 9 . . . .] κ̣ατ̣[ὰ]
[- . . . 7 . . . κ]αὶ τῶν
[- . . . . 8 . . . .] τοῦ δή-
[μου -] *vacat*

24. Reinmuth 1971, p. 133.

a

b

Figure 23. Fragments of a decree perhaps concerning *epheboi?* (23): (a) fr. *a*, I 4902c; (b) fr. *b*, I 4902d

Fragment *a*, line 1: The mason at first omitted the omega, then corrected his mistake by erasing the nu and carving omega inter-stoichos, its right half overlaying the faint traces of the erasure of the nu.

Line 6: The base of a right diagonal is visible before the epsilon.

Line 7: The base of a right diagonal appears before the tau.

Line 9: The apex of a triangular letter survives at the left edge.

Fragment *b*, line 1: The tip of the lower diagonal of kappa (or chi?), the lower half of alpha, and the base of a central vertical are preserved.

The lettering suggests a date in the late 330s or the 320s B.C.

These fragments may derive from an ephebic decree, and, if so, the line length will have been considerable.

24 Fragment of a decree — Fig. 24

I 4982. A fragment of a stele of pale yellowish-white Hymettian(?) marble discovered on June 16, 1937, on the north slope of the Acropolis (T 26–27), in the original filling of the Post-Herulian Wall over the paved court below Klepsydra. The right side, flat top, and back are preserved, with a crowning molding, cavetto, and horizontal taenia. The vertical space between the first line of the inscription and the bottom of the molding is 0.04.

H. 0.11, W. 0.19, Th. 0.115 (projection of molding and taenia 0.035); L.H. 0.005; stoich. 0.01 (square).

Slightly before 321/20 B.C.? — Stoich.

[ἐπὶ - - - - - - ἄρχοντος], ἐπὶ τῆ[ς]
[- - - - - - - - - - - - - - - - - . . .]Ṇ[. .]
[- -]

Line 2: Below the tau of line 1 the top of a right hasta is visible in the break, perhaps part of a nu or eta.

Figure 24. Fragment of a decree (24)

25 Fragment of a proxeny decree for Sostratos of Herakleia Fig. 25

I 2805. A fragment of a relief stele of Pentelic marble discovered on April 18, 1935, over the back foundation and east side of the East Building (P 14), in Early Byzantine fill. It is broken all around and on the back, but parts of a crowning molding, horizontal inscribed taenia, and the lower right part of a deeply cut relief are preserved.

H. 0.11 (stele face 0.009, molding 0.025, taenia 0.025, relief 0.051), W. 0.062, Th. 0.052; L.H. 0.009; non-stoich., four letters occupy a horizontal space of 0.036.

Ca. 320 B.C.? Non-stoich.

Προξενία Σωστρ[άτωι - - -] Ἡρακ[λεώτηι]

The text of the new fragment is underlined.

Alpha is unusually wide, its horizontal sloping slightly up to the right, and rho has a very wide loop whose height is half the height of the vertical.

The dimensions of the taenia, the depth of the relief, the letter height, and the shapes of alpha and rho are the same as those of *IG* II^2 419 (EM 7221), the honorific decree for the *proxenos* Sostratos, and this fragment surely derives from the same stele.

Figure 25. Fragment of a proxeny decree for Sostratos of Herakleia (25)

The fragment of the relief surviving on I 2805 preserves the lower right edge of the hem of a robe, broken diagonally from lower left to upper right, and matching the breakage on the lower right edge of the robe of a larger, central figure whose left part is preserved on *IG* II^2 419, the Goddess Athena, who stands facing Herakles, probably the hero of Sostratos's hometown, as Lawton notes.[25] The edges of both stones, however, are so worn and battered that a clear join cannot be achieved.[26] Therefore,

25. Lawton 1995, p. 150, no. 158; photograph, pl. 83. That Sostratos was a citizen of Herakleia was first suggested by Koehler (see *IG* II 5 200c). Lawton dates the relief to the last quarter of the 4th century. For further bibliography on *IG* II^2 419, see Culasso Gastaldi 2004, p. 257.

26. It has not been possible to take the Agora fragment to the Epigraphic Museum, but I made a plasticine and plaster cast of its edge in 2002 and attempted, unsuccessfully, to fit this onto the edge of *IG* II^2 419.

if the fragments do not join, there may or may not be more text between them, hence my dashes: there could be another name, for instance, or a patronymic.

Line 1: Προξενία Σωστρ[άτου - - - Ἡρακλεώτου?] *IG* II 5 200c; Σωστρ[άτωι . . ca. 6 . . Ἡρακλεώτηι] Culasso Gastaldi 2004, p. 257.

26 Fragments of a decree conferring citizenship? Fig. 26

I 5778, I 5707. Two nonjoining fragments of a stele of micaceous Pentelic marble discovered at different times and places.

Fragment *a* (I 5778) was discovered on April 20, 1939, west of the Panathenaic Way, southwest of the Eleusinion (S 22), in a Late Roman context. It is broken all around and on the back.

H. 0.125, W. 0.06, Th. 0.06; L.H. 0.007–0.008; stoich. hor. 0.017, vert. 0.02.

Fragment *b* (I 5707) was discovered on March 7, 1939, in the area between the north slope of the Acropolis and that of the Areopagus (P–S 22–24), in a modern house wall. The smooth-dressed right side is preserved, with a margin of 0.027. The back has been reworked.

H. 0.113, W. 0.066, Th. 0.053; L.H. 0.007–0.008; stoich. vert. 0.018.

Ca. 334–320 B.C. Stoich.

a

[- -]
[- - - - - . . 5 . .]P[- - - - - - - - - -]
[- - - - - - - . . . .]Λ̣Α[- - - - - - - - - -]
[- - - - - - - . . . .]ΝΠ[- - - - - - - - - -]
[- - - - - δεδό]χθ[αι - - - - - - - -]
[- - - - - - - . . . .]ΕΝ[- - - - - - - - - -]
[- - - - - . . 5 . .]Λ[- - - - - - - - - -]
[- -]

b

[- -]
[- -]P
[- -]K
[- -]E
[- -]Ṇ
[- -]

Fragment *a,* line 2: The base of a right diagonal survives before the alpha.

Fragment *b,* line 4: The top of the second vertical of eta, or nu, survives.

This fragment should derive from near the bottom of its stele, to judge by its wide margin.

These fragments have the same type of marble, lettering, and spacing as the 11 fragments published as *Agora* XVI, no. 94,[27] and may be yet more members of this group.[28]

27. Photographs of the fragments of *Agora* XVI, no. 94: Schweigert 1939, pp. 27–30, no. 7; 1940, pp. 335–339, no. 42.

28. Tracy (*ADT,* pp. 120–128; description of lettering, pp. 120–121; photograph, p. 121, fig. 9) attributes *Agora* XVI, no. 94, to his "Cutter of EM 12807," active between 334/3 and 314/3 B.C. For the most recent edition of *Agora* XVI, no. 94, see Lambert 2001a; he separates 10 fragments into two groups, one having a line of 28 letters and dated to 323/2 B.C., the other of 26 letters and dated between 334 and 320 B.C. He rejects the eleventh fragment, *k,* altogether.

a b

Figure 26. Fragments of a decree conferring citizenship? (**26**): (a) fr. *a*, I 5778; (b) fr. *b*, I 5707

27 Fragment of a decree conferring citizenship — Fig. 27

I 4524. A fragment of a stele of micaceous Pentelic marble discovered on February 17, 1937, in a modern cellar wall on the north slope of the Areopagus (K 17). The pick-dressed right side and rough-picked back are preserved; the right margin is 0.014.

H. 0.174, W. 0.074, Th. 0.091; L.H. 0.006; stoich. 0.0146 (square).

Ca. 330–320 B.C.? — Stoich. 24

[- -]
[- - - - - - - - - - - - - - - - - -]ΑΠΕ
[. . Ἀθηναῖον καὶ ἐκγόνου]ς καὶ
[γράψασθαι φυλῆς καὶ δήμ]ου κα-
[ὶ φρατρίας ἧς ἂν βούληται]ι κατ-
[ὰ τὸν νόμον· τοὺς δὲ πρυτά]νεις̣
[τῆς . . .6. . . ίδος δοῦναι π]ερὶ α̣-
[ὐτοῦ τὴν ψῆφον εἰς τὴν πρ]ώτ̣[ην]
[ἐκκλησίαν καὶ τοὺς θεσμ]οθ̣[έτ]-
[ας δοκιμάσαι τὴν πολιτε]ί̣[αν ὅ]-
[ταν πρῶτον χρῶνται δικαστηρ]-
[ίοις κτλ. - - - - - - - - - - - - - - - -]

Line 5: The lower right corner of nu survives in the first stoichos in the abrasion. In the fourth, the left end of the top diagonal of sigma is preserved.

Line 6: The left diagonal of alpha is barely visible in the abrasion.

Line 8: There is a trace of the top of a circular letter after the omicron.

Line 9: The top of a central vertical is visible below the omicron of line 8.

Spacing and letters are virtually identical to those of *IG* II^2 270 (EM 2613), apparently dated late in the 320s B.C., but the line length is different.[29] Most of the letter forms found on this fragment appear also on *IG* II^2 270, with the exception of kappa, but the hand of both documents is less regular than it appears at first: the mason, for instance, used the same chisel for all three strokes of alpha, so that the horizontal extends some distance to the left of the left diagonal. The diagonals of

Figure 27. Fragment of a decree conferring citizenship (**27**)

29. On the date of *IG* II^2 270, see Walbank 2002, pp. 63–64, no. 6.

kappa are angled rather narrowly and do not quite meet the vertical; and upsilon is made with a short vertical and two longer diagonals. On both fragments there is also some variation in individual letters. The physical similarities between this document and *IG* II² 270 indicate that it should be of about the same date, even though it is certainly part of a different inscription.

Line 2: The restoration in line 4, which seems inevitable, implies that a single honorand is involved and was probably present in Athens at the time of the passage of this decree.

Lines 6–11: For this restoration cf. *IG* II² 398b, lines 2–6.[30]

28 Fragment of a decree Fig. 28

I 5848. A fragment of a stele of micaceous Pentelic marble discovered on May 24, 1939, in the area between the north slope of the Acropolis and that of the Areopagus (Q–R 23–24), in a modern wall. The pick-dressed right side is preserved, with a right margin increasing from 0.007 to 0.009, top to bottom.

H. 0.17, W. 0.065, Th. 0.07; L.H. 0.006–0.007; stoich. hor. 0.015, vert. 0.0146.

Ca. 330–320 B.C.? Stoich.

[- - - - - - - - - - - - - - - -]
[- - - - - - - - - - - . . ⁵ . .]Α̣Σ
[- - - - - - - - - - - - . . . .]Λ̣ΙΟ
[- - - - - - - - - - - - . . . .]ΕΣΑ
[- - - - - - - - - - - - . . . .]ΙΕΔ
[- - - - - - - - - - τῶι] δήμω-
[ι - - - - - - - - - - - . . .]ΤΟΥΔ
[- - - - - - - - - - - - . . .]ΤΕΛΕ
[- - - - - - - - - - - - . . .]ΑΥΤΟ
[- - - - - - - - - - - - . . . .]<Α>ΝΕ
[- - - - - - - - - - - - . . .]ΕΡΑΤ
[- - - - - - - - - - - - . . . .]ΕΡ̣Ο̣
[- - - - - - - - - - - - - - - -]

Line 1: The base of the right diagonal of alpha survives.

Line 2: The base of the right diagonal of alpha or lambda is preserved in the break.

Line 9: The right half of the first stoichos is uninscribed, so that an iota is likely to have been cut here. The first preserved letter is surely an alpha, but the crossbar has been omitted.

Line 11: The vertical and upper part of the loop of rho survive, but the stone is so abraded that it is not possible to rule out a beta here. The top of a circular letter appears to survive in the abraded area to right of this.

I believe that the hand is close to that of *IG* II² 270 (EM 2613), which provides an approximate date in the 320s B.C.;[31] note especially the shapes of alpha, epsilon, mu, rho, sigma, upsilon, and omega.

Lines 4–6: [Ειτεα]ῖ(ος) (= Phyle X)· ἔδ|[οξεν τῆι βουλῆι καὶ τῶι] δήμω|[ι]? If this is correct, the prescript will have contained a list of eight *symproedroi*,[32] named with abbreviated demotics and without patronymics, likely in the official order of phylai, followed by the usual formula for a decision of the Boule and the Demos, which provides the line length of 23 letters.

Figure 28. Fragment of a decree (28)

30. *IG* II² 398b = *Naturalization* I, D36.

31. See n. 29, above.

32. See n. 18, above.

Figure 29. Fragments of a decree (29): (a) fr. *a*, I 5838; (b) fr. *b*, I 6777

a b

29 Fragments of a decree Fig. 29

I 5838, I 6777. Two fragments of a stele of slightly micaceous Pentelic marble discovered at different times and places. There is no join, but the physical appearance of these fragments, as well as the closeness of their findspots, makes it highly likely that they derive from the same stele.

Fragment *a* (I 5838) was discovered on May 20, 1939, between the north slope of the Acropolis and that of the Areopagus (R 22), in a modern wall. It is broken all around and on the back. The face still bears the vertical marks of the finishing rasp.

H. 0.15, W. 0.10, Th. 0.06.

Fragment *b* (I 6777) was discovered in April of 1957, outside the Market Square and west of the Panathenaic Way (P 20:2), in a well of Early Roman context. It is broken all around and on the back. The face still bears the vertical marks of the finishing rasp.

H. 0.11, W. 0.082, Th. 0.046.

Both fragments: L.H. 0.008–0.009; stoich. hor. 0.02, vert. 0.0175.

Ca. 334–313 B.C.? Stoich.

a
[- -]
[. . . . Γ]α̣μ[ηλίωνος - - - - - - - - - - - - - - - - - - -]
[τῆς πρ]υτα̣[νείας· - - - - - - - - - - - - - - - - - - -]
[. . . . τ]ῶν π[ροέδρων ἐ]πε[ψήφιζεν - - - - - - - -] *b*
[. . . 6 . . .]ΥΑ[. . . ἔδοξε]ν Τ[- - - - - - - - - - - - - - -]
[. . . 6 . . .]Ο̣Υ̣[. . . . 8 . . . .] ε̣ἶπ[εν - - - - - - - - - - - -]
[. . . . . 16 . . . .]ΛΗΣ[- - - - - - - - - - - - - - -]
[. . . . . 16 . . . .]ΙΩΝ[- - - - - - - - - - - - - - -]
[. . . . . 17 . . . .]Μ̣Υ̣[- - - - - - - - - - - - - - -]
[- -]

Line 1: The base of a right diagonal is followed by the outline of a mu in the abrasion.

Line 2: The base of the left diagonal of alpha survives.

Line 3: On fragment *b*, the second vertical and part of the horizontal of pi are visible.

Line 4: On fragment *a*, the horizontal of alpha is set so low that this letter might well be read as a delta.

Line 5: On fragment *a* the upper right quadrant of a circular letter is followed by the top of the left diagonal of an upsilon or chi. On fragment *b* the right end of the lowest horizontal of epsilon survives.

Line 8: A right apex, probably that of a mu, is followed by the top of a left diagonal.

The shapes of nu, sigma, upsilon, and omega, and the tendency to thicken the free ends of letter strokes, suggest to me that the hand may be that of the "Cutter of EM 12807."[33]

30 Fragment of a decree concerning the repair of the fortification walls of Athens — Fig. 30

I 4544. A fragment of a stele of Pentelic marble discovered on February 26, 1937, under Acropolis Street, west of the Post-Herulian Wall (R–S 25), in a modern context. It is broken all around and on the back. It joins the upper left edge of Agora I 3843, and thus probably also the bottom right edge of the fragment EM 10396 (= *IG* II² 463), linking lines 93–101 of the composite stele *Agora* XVI, no. 109.[34]

H. 0.15, W. 0.10, Th. 0.065; L.H. 0.006–0.007; stoich. 0.0125 (square).

307/6 B.C. Stoich. 71

ΤΙΣ[. . .]ΣΑΙΑΡΡΟΟ[. . .]Σ [ἀ]ποφορήσ[ε]ι *v* τὸν χοῦν οὗ ἂν γ[ί]γ[νητα]⟦ι Η⟧[. . . . . 20 . . . . τ]-
οῦ <κ>[ύκλ]ο̣υ̣? ἃς παρ[έξου]σιν δέκα, τὸν χ̣άρακα [.]ΠΙ[. .]ΑΜ[. .]Ο[. . . .]Ι̣ΝΕΙ̣[. . . . . 20 . . . .]
ΩΣ[. . . . .] παραλα[βών· ἅ]μ[α] δ[ὲ] τὰς ὁδοὺς τὰς [ἐ]ν τ[οῖ]ς μα[κρ]ο[ῖς] τείχε[σι . . . . 19 . . . .]
ΜΟ[. .] ἑκάστω [.]Κ[. . . 7 . . .]Ο[. .]ΤΟ[.]ΑΟ[.]ΥΡΟ[.] ὃ ἂν [μι]σθώση̣τ[αι] τ⟦ε̣⟧ίχ⟦η⟧
[. . . . . 21 . . . .]
Υ [ἑκα]τ̣έρου πα[ραστή]σ[ουσι κ]α[ὶ τ]ὸν χάρακα [π]α[ρὰ] τὸν Πε[ιρ]αιέα ΛΗ̣[. . . . . 21 . . . .]
ΕΙ[.]Ω[. .]Ω[. . 5 . . τὰ τε]ίχη [π]ά[ν]τ[α ἐ]ξεργασ[άμε]νοι Ο[. . . 7 . . .] Τ̣ΡΙΓΩ[. . . . 11 . . . . . τοὺς μεμισθ]-
ωμένους κ[αὶ περὶ τοῦ] κεράμο[υ] ὅσομ παρ[έλ]αβον . . 5 . .] ΕΔΟΥΛ̣[. . . . . 21 . . . .]
[.]Α[.]ΟΝ[.]Ι[. . . . 10 . . . . .]ΜΕΝΟ[. . . .]ΝΑΝΜΗ[. . .]ΔΕΝΑ[. . . . 9 . . . .]ΗΝΗΙ̣ΠΤΙ̣[. . . . . 19 . . . .]
δὲ αὐ̣το[. . . 6 . . .]Ν̣[. . . .] εἴ τις [. . .]ΑΟΙΔΕΙ[. .]ΛΗΦ[. . . . 8 . . . . ἀ]πὸ τῶν τει[χῶν . . . . 15 . . . .]

The text of the new fragment is underlined.

Line 93 (lines 93–101 = lines 1–9 of I 4544): The mason first omitted the iota of γίγνηται and then inserted it inter-stoichos; the following eta is roughly engraved, perhaps a correction of another mistake.

Line 94: The bases of two central verticals survive in the first and fourth stoichoi, respectively.

Line 95: The lower left corner of the second epsilon survives.

Line 96: In the second stoichos the mason engraved an omicron, which he then corrected to a faint epsilon; in the fifth stoichos he engraved an epsilon, then corrected this to an eta.

Line 97: In the first stoichos the base of a right diagonal survives, followed by the base of a central vertical; in the fifth and sixth stoichoi a lambda is followed by the left side of an eta or epsilon: the top and the bottom of the vertical and the surface to right of it are not preserved.

Line 98: The right tip of the horizontal of a tau or gamma survives, followed by a rho with a squarish loop. In the fifth stoichos the left horizontal extender of omega is visible, but no part of its loop.

Line 99: The left diagonal and apex of a triangular letter survive in the fifth stoichos; the bottom of this stoichos is damaged, making it uncertain whether this letter is a lambda or a delta.

33. See n. 28, above.

34. Autopsy confirms the join with Agora I 3843, which is still in the Agora storage area, but it has not been possible to take the new Agora fragment to the Epigraphic Museum.

Figure 30. Fragment of a decree concerning the repair of the fortification walls of Athens (30)

Line 100: The top of a central vertical survives after the second eta.

Line 101: After the omicron the middle part of the vertical and the left end of the horizontal of tau survive.

The above restorations are based upon Maier's revision of *IG* II² 463, lines 93–101.[35]

31 Fragment of a decree in honor of a citizen of Herakleia? Fig. 31

I 1644. A fragment of a stele of Hymettian marble discovered on March 24, 1934, over the floor of the Tholos (G 11), in an Ottoman context. It is broken all around and on the back.

H. 0.084, W. 0.082, Th. 0.074; L.H. 0.007; non-stoich. vert. 0.0115–0.013.

Figure 31. Fragment of a decree in honor of a citizen of Herakleia? (31)

Ca. 305/4 B.C.? Non-stoich.

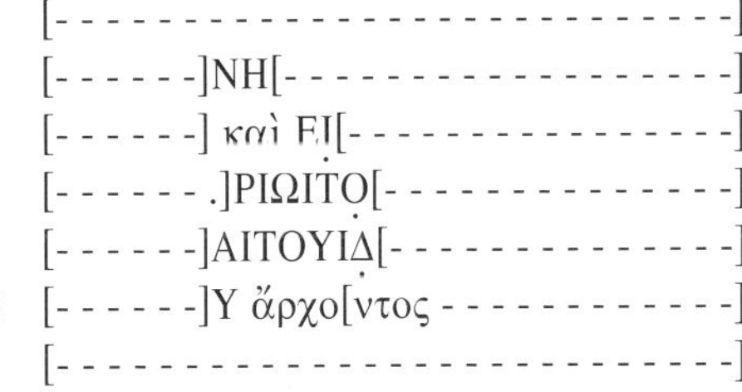

[- -]
[- - - - - -]NH[- - - - - - - - - - - - - - - - - - -]
[- - - - - -] καὶ ΕỊ[- - - - - - - - - - - - - - - - -]
[- - - - - - .]ΡΙΩΙΤΟ̣[- - - - - - - - - - - - - - -]
[- - - - - -]ΑΙΤΟΥΙΔ̣[- - - - - - - - - - - - - - -]
[- - - - - -]Υ ἄρχο[ν̣τος - - - - - - - - - - - - -]
[- -]

Line 1: After nu the lower part of the left vertical and part of the horizontal of eta survive; an apparent horizontal stroke at the base of the vertical is much shallower and is probably merely a random mark.

35. Maier 1959, pp. 48–67, no. 11, the basis for the text printed as *Agora* XVI, no. 109.

Line 2: The base of a vertical is visible in the break to the right of the epsilon.

Line 3: The bottom of a round letter survives after tau.

Line 4: After the second iota there is a diagonal stroke, with a possible horizontal joining it at its base: if this is a letter stroke, the letter is certainly a delta.

The shapes of alpha, kappa, nu, omicron, rho, upsilon, and omega are identical to those of *IG* II^2 479 (EM 7284), and the spacing and marble are the same.[36] It is likely that this fragment derives from the same stele, but there is no join.

Line 3: [ἐν βουλευτη]ρίωι?
Line 4: [κ]αὶ τοῦ ἰδ̣[ίου]?
Line 5: An archon date? Cf. *IG* II^2 479, lines 4 and 12.

32 Fragment of a decree concerning sacrifice and thanksgiving for the successful campaign of Demetrios Poliorketes — Fig. 32

I 3836. A fragment of a stele of Pentelic marble discovered on March 19, 1936, in the southeast part of the Market Square (K–Q 14–17), in a marble dump. It is broken all around, and the back has been reworked and cut down. It belongs between fragments *a* and *b* of *Agora* XVI, no. 114, corresponding to lines 9–14 of the composite document.

H. 0.14, W. 0.12, Th. 0.068; L.H. 0.005; stoich. 0.01 (square).

304/3 B.C. — Stoich. 36

[κα]-
ὶ αὐτονόμους πεπόηκεν· ὅ[πως ἄν οὗ]<u>ν κα̣ὶ̣ τ̣</u>[ὰ λοι]-
πὰ συντελῆται ἐπὶ τῶι συ[μφέρο]<u>ντ</u>[ι] <u>τῶι τ</u>[ε δήμ]-
[ω]ι τῶι Ἀθηναίων καὶ τοῖς [βασιλ]<u>ε̣ῦσι̣ν̣ κ</u>[αὶ οἱ σ]-
[τ]ρατευόμενοι σωιζόμεν[οι . . . .]<u>Τ̣ΕΣ</u>[. . κατίω]-
[σ]ιν εἰς τὴν πόλιν κρατήσ[αντες .]<u>ΟΥΠ̣</u>[. . . ^{7} . . .]
[β]οῦς θῦσαι τοὺς πρυτάνε[ις τῆς Ἀκα]<u>μ̣</u>[αντίδος]

The text of the new fragment is underlined.

Line 9 (= line 1 of I 3836): The bases of the diagonals of alpha and of the verticals of iota and tau are preserved.

Line 10: In the first stoichos, nu is complete; it is followed by the faint outline of a tau.

Line 11: The tips of the upper and lower horizontals of epsilon survive; the tops of iota and of the left hasta of nu are visible after sigma, followed by a kappa.

Line 12: The right tip of the horizontal of tau is preserved, followed by a faint epsilon.

Line 13: The upper left corner of pi survives.

Line 14: The top of the first apex of mu is preserved below the upsilon of line 13.

Autopsy makes it plain that the physical characteristics of this fragment exactly match those of *Agora* XVI, no. 114,[37] but there is no join.

The restorations of the ends of lines 11, 12, and 13 offered in *Agora* XVI are no longer valid.

Line 11: Habicht's suggestion for this line is confirmed.[38]

Line 12: [κατέλθω|σιν] Ferguson 1948, p. 114; [κατίω|σιν] *Agora* XVI; [ἅπαν]τὲς [κατέλθω|σιν] or [ἅπαν]τές [τε κατίω|σιν]?

Line 14: [τ]οῦ π̣[ολεμίου]?

36. Tracy (*ADT,* pp. 164–169) attributes *IG* II^2 479 to the "Cutter of Agora I 4266," active between ca. 304 and 271 B.C.; photograph of I 4266, p. 165, fig. 18.

37. Discussion and photographs of both fragments of *Agora* XVI, no. 114: Meritt 1947, p. 153, no. 46, pl. XXVI; and Ferguson 1948, pp. 114–136, no. 68, pl. 33.

38. Habicht 1990.

Figure 32. Fragment of a decree concerning sacrifice and thanksgiving for the successful campaign of Demetrios Poliorketes (32)

Figure 33. Fragment of a decree conferring citizenship upon Neaios (33)

33 Fragment of a decree conferring citizenship upon Neaios Fig. 33

I 1425. A fragment of a stele of micaceous Pentelic marble discovered on March 2, 1934, just outside the Tholos, on the north (G 11), in a late context. It is broken all around and on the back. This fragment appears to be part of *IG* II[2] 553, lines 5–9, but there is no actual join.

H. 0.088, W. 0.014, Th. 0.045; L.H. 0.005; stoich. vert. 0.01.

304/3 B.C.? Stoich. 39

[Νικοκ]λείδου τοῦ στρατη[γο]ῦ καὶ [οἱ . . . ⁷ . . .]Π̲[. . .]
[. . .]ΟΥ καὶ ταῦτα πρότερό[ν τ]ε ἐπέ[στειλεν Νι]κ̲[οκλ]-
[είδ]ης περὶ Νεαίου τῆι βου̣[λ]ῆι καὶ τ̣[ῶι δήμωι] κ̲[αὶ ν]-
[ῦ]ν̣ παρὼν αὐτὸς ἀποφαίνει τ̣ῶι δήμω[ι πολλοῖ]ς̣ [καί]-
ροις ἔτι προσεπέδωκε Νεα̣ῖος τῶι δή[μωι δωρ]ε̲[ὰς ε]-
ἰς τὸν πόλεμον κτλ. -]

The text of the new fragment is underlined.

Line 5 (= line 1 of I 1425): The first vertical of pi is concealed by a deep abrasion, but the second vertical and a faint trace of the horizontal are preserved.

The ends of these lines were left unrestored by Osborne, the most recent editor of this text,[39] whose edition and dating I have used here. The new fragment provides a name (line 6), a context (line 8) and the nature of Neaios's benefactions (line 9).

39. *Naturalization* I, pp. 113–114; II, pp. 117–120, D44.

Figure 34. Fragment of a decree conferring citizenship (34)

34 Fragment of a decree conferring citizenship Fig. 34

I 5894. A fragment of a stele of yellow-flecked, pale gray Hymettian marble discovered on May 22, 1940, among marbles from the area of the Hephaisteion (C–G 5–10). It is broken all around, but the rough-picked back is preserved. The face still bears marks of the finishing rasp, running diagonally from top left to bottom right.

H. 0.112, W. 0.085, Th. 0.064; L.H. 0.006–0.007; stoich. hor. 0.011, vert. 0.0114.

Ca. 307–304 B.C.? Stoich. 25

[- -]
[. . . . .11. . . . .]Δ[. . . . . .13. . . . . .]
[. . . . .10. . . . .]ΕΥ[. . . . . .13. . . . . .]
[. . . .8. . . .]ΣΕΙΣΤ[. . . . . .12. . . . . .]-
[. . .6. . . κ]αὶ τοὺς [. . . . .9. . . . καὶ]-
[στεφανῶ]σαι ἕκα[στον αὐτῶν χρυ]-
[σῶι στεφ]άνωι ἀ̣π[ὸ Χ ? δραχμῶν· εἶν]-
[αι δὲ αὐτο]ὺς κα̣[ὶ Ἀθηναίους καὶ]
[ἐξεῖναι αὐ]το̣[ῖς γράψασθαι φυλ]-
[ῆς καὶ δήμου καὶ φρατρίας κτλ. -]

Line 1: The lower left corner of a delta survives above the upsilon of line 2.

Line 3: The right tips of the diagonals of sigma survive in the first stoichos.

Line 5: The upper and lower horizontals of epsilon are visible at the edges of a deep abrasion.

Line 6: In the first stoichos the stone breaks on the right diagonal of alpha; in the sixth, the upper left corner of pi survives.

Line 8: The upper left curve of a circular letter survives after tau.

The lettering seems appropriate to the end of the 4th or the beginning of the 3rd century B.C.

Lines 3–4: εἰς τ[ὸν δῆμον τὸν Ἀθη|ναίων κ]αὶ τοὺς [συμμάχους]?

Line 6: The formula for the cost of the crown places this decree in or before 304/3 B.C.[40]

Line 8: For [ἐξεῖναι], rather than [εἶναι], cf. *IG* II² 511, line 2; 570, line 5; and 654, lines 47–48.

35 Fragment of an honorific decree — Fig. 35

I 4533. A fragment of a stele of slightly micaceous Pentelic marble discovered on February 27, 1937, in the area southeast of the Market Square, east of the Post-Herulian Wall (T–U 22), in a Byzantine context. It is broken all around and on the back.

H. 0.121, W. 0.04, Th. 0.035; L.H. 0.008; stoich. 0.016 (square).

Ca. 303–302 B.C.? — Stoich.

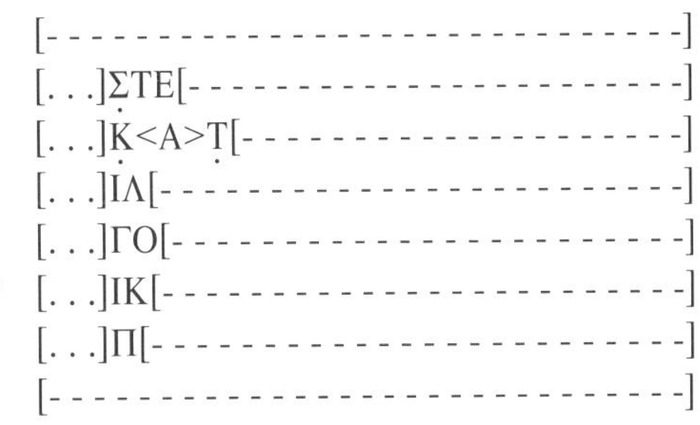

[- -]
[. . .]Σ̣ΤΕ[- -]
[. . .]Ḳ<Α>Ṭ[- - - - - - - - - - - - - - - - - - -]
[. . .]ΙΛ[- -]
[. . .]Γ̣Ο[- -]
[. . .]ΙΚ[- -]
[. . .]Π[- -]
[- -]

Line 1: The right tip of the lowest diagonal of sigma survives.

Line 2: The tips of both diagonals of kappa and the left tip of the horizontal of tau are preserved. The alpha lacks a crossbar.

Line 4: The base of the vertical and the right tip of the horizontal of gamma are visible.

The letter forms, spacing, and marble appear to be the same as those of *Agora* XVI, no. 127 (I 5824), placed by its editor a little before 302/1 B.C.,[41] but the lettering is shallower.

Line 1: στε̣[φανῶσαι]?

Lines 1–2: [χρυσῶι στεφά|νωι] κ̣<α>τ̣[ὰ τὸν νόμον]? If this is correct, reference to the law limiting the price of gold crowns (line 2) dates this document to the end of 304/3 B.C. or later.[42]

Figure 35. Fragment of an honorific decree (35)

36 Fragment from the conclusion of a decree — Fig. 36

I 5627. A fragment of a stele of Pentelic marble discovered on October 14, 1938, in a modern house wall at the north foot of the Areopagus (P 23). The sharply undercut right side is preserved, along with the rough-picked back.

H. 0.135, W. 0.08, Th. 0.066; L.H. 0.006–0.007; stoich. hor. 0.012, vert. 0.0125.

40. *IG* II² 484 is probably the top portion of the decree in honor of Oxythemis of Larisa (*IG* II² 558) and, if so, the decree is dated to 304/3 B.C., and the date of the introduction of the law limiting the cost of golden crowns is more precisely fixed than previously had been thought, that is, before Prytany VIII of 304/3 B.C.; see Walbank 1990, pp. 445–446, no. 20 (= *SEG* XL 83).

41. Tracy (*ADT*, pp. 120–128) places *Agora* XVI, no. 127, at ca. 325 B.C.; Woodhead (*Agora* XVI) makes a convincing case for a much later date (see also **36**, below).

42. See n. 40, above.

302/1 B.C.? Stoich. 27

[- -]
[. . . . . .23. . . . .]Α̣Ι̣[. .]
[. . . . . .23. . . . .]ΑΘΗΝ
[. . . . . .23. . . . .]ΙΝΑΙ
[. . . . . .23. . . . .]ΝΑΘΗ
[. . . . . .23. . . . .]Ν ὅτι
[ὁ δῆμος τιμᾶι τοὺς δεικνυμέ]νους
[αὐτῶι τὴν εὔνοιαν· ἀναγράψα]ι δὲ τ-
[όδε τὸ ψήφισμα τὸν γραμματέα] τὸν
[κατὰ πρυτανείαν ἐστήλην λιθί]νη̣-
[ν κτλ. - - - - - - - - - - - - - - - - - - -]

Figure 36. Fragment from the conclusion of a decree (36)

Line 1: The bases of the diagonals of alpha and the base of iota survive.
Line 3: The last two letters are badly damaged, but certain.
Line 9: The top of the left vertical of eta survives.

This fragment is part of the same stele as *Agora* XVI, no. 125 (I 707),[43] but does not join it. On both fragments the right side deeply undercuts the face: when the angles of undercutting are compared, they match precisely. The back of each is rough-picked, with a pattern of nearly vertical chisel strokes, each made with a blade ca. 0.015–0.020 wide. I 5627 is thicker than I 707 and its right margin increases from top to bottom, from 0.022 to 0.024, while that of I 707 increases from 0.018 to 0.019; these features are to be expected when the stele tapers in both axes, as this one does. Each fragment is restorable with a line of 27 letters, and their spacing, letter shapes, and marble are identical.

Lines 1–5: [εἶν]α̣ι̣ [δὲ |καὶ γῆς καὶ οἰκίας ἔγκτησιν] Ἀθήν|[ησι αὐτῶι καὶ ἐκγόνοις καὶ ε]ἶναι |[αὐτοῖς ἰσοτέλειαν οἰκοῦσι]ν Ἀθή|[νησι ὅπως ἂν οἱ ἄλλοι εἰδῶσι]ν?

37 Fragment of an honorific decree Fig. 37

I 2764. A fragment of a stele of micaceous Pentelic marble discovered on April 9, 1935, over the Middle Stoa terrace, at the east end (N–O 12), in a late context. The pick-dressed right side is preserved; the back is flat and rough-picked, and may be original.

H. 0.19, W. 0.168, Th. 0.102; L.H. 0.005; semi-stoich. hor. 0.011, vert. 0.013.

Ca. 307–301 B.C.? Semi-stoich. 38?

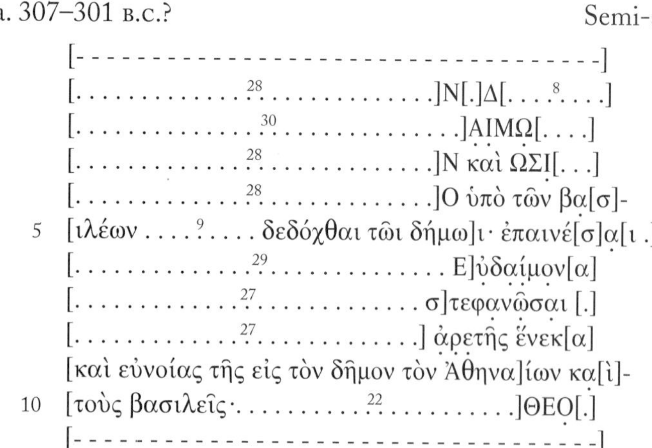

[- -]
[. . . . . .28. . . . .]Ν[.]Δ[. . . .8. . . .]
[. . . . . .30. . . . .]Α̣Ι̣ΜΩ[. . . .]
[. . . . . .28. . . . .]Ν καὶ ΩΣΙ̣[. . .]
[. . . . . .28. . . . .]Ο ὑπὸ τῶν βα̣[σ]-
[ιλέων . . . .9. . . . δεδόχθαι τῶι δήμω]ι· ἐπαινέ[σ]α̣[ι .]
[. . . . . .29. . . . . Ε]ὐ̣δα̣ίμον[α]
[. . . . . .27. . . . . σ]τεφανῶσαι [.]
[. . . . . .27. . . . .] ἀρετῆς ἕνεκ[α]
[καὶ εὐνοίας τῆς εἰς τὸν δῆμον τὸν Ἀθηνα]ίων κα̣[ὶ]-
[τοὺς βασιλεῖς·. . . . . .22. . . . .]ΘΕΟ̣[.]
[- -]

43. Photograph of *Agora* XVI, no. 125: Oliver 1935, p. 37, no. 6. This decree was probably passed in Prytany X of 302/1 B.C., but the date is in dispute; for a summary of the arguments and counterarguments, see *Agora* XVI, pp. 198–199.

Figure 37. Fragment of an honorific decree (37)

The stoichedon order is much disturbed: lines 7, 8, and 9 appear to be set off half a stoichos to the right of lines 1, 2, 4, 5, and 6, and individual letters do not always line up vertically with those above or below them.

Line 2: In the first stoichos the faint outlines of what may be an alpha and an iota are visible in the abraded area; in the fourth, a circular letter survives; its flat base suggests that it is not an omicron but an omega whose horizontal extenders extend into the letter, closing it off.

Line 3: A vertical stroke is visible at the right, but not enough is preserved to say whether this is an iota or some other letter such as epsilon or eta.

Line 4: Part of the lower loop of beta survives, followed by the bases of the diagonals of a triangular letter.

Line 5: The bases of the diagonals of the second alpha survive.

Line 6: Traces here are the tip of the right diagonal of upsilon, a clear delta, the outline of a triangular letter, probably alpha, the top of a central vertical, probably iota, the upper half of mu, the upper curve of omicron, and part of the diagonal and the top of the right hasta of nu.

Line 7: After phi the diagonals of alpha, a faint nu, the upper curve of omega, parts of all four diagonals of sigma, and the apex of the second alpha survive.

Line 8: The apex of alpha, the upper part of the loop of rho, and the upper left corner of epsilon are visible, though badly abraded.

Line 9: The apex of alpha survives.

Line 10: Below and between the nu and kappa of line 9 is a theta, followed by a faint epsilon and another circular letter.

Line 1: [ἐκ τῶ]ν [ἰ]δ[ίων]?

Line 2: [Εὐδ]α̣ί̣μω̣[ν]? Perhaps the honorand of line 6.

Lines 4–5: Mention of the kings indicates a date of 307–301 B.C.

Line 8: Because of the irregular stoichedon pattern, the restorations [ἀπὸ Χ δραχμῶν] and [κατὰ τὸν νόμον] are both possible; the former would place this document in or before 304/3 B.C., when the law limiting the cost of gold crowns was introduced.[44]

38 Fragment of a decree Fig. 38

I 4484. A fragment of a stele of blue-gray Hymettian marble discovered on February 5, 1937, in front of the south end of the Stoa of Attalos (P 11), in a modern context. It is broken all around and on the back.

H. 0.079, W. 0.061, Th. 0.099; L.H. 0.005–0.006; stoich. 0.013 (square).

End of 4th century B.C. Stoich.

vacat

[ἐπὶ - - - - - - ἄρχοντος, ἐπὶ τῆς - - - -]ΕΙΔ[- - - πρυτανείας, ἧι - - - - - - -]
[- - - - - - ἐγραμμάτευεν, - - - - - - - - -]ΤΗΡ̣[- - - - - - τῆς πρυτανείας, ἐκ]-
[κλησία· τῶν προέδρων ἐπεψήφιζεν -]ΗΙΠ[- - - - - - - - - - - - - - - - - καὶ]
[συμπρόεδροι· ἔδοξεν τῆι βουλῆι· - -]Α̣Ν[- - - - - - - - - - - - - - - - εἶπεν]
[- -]

Figure 38. Fragment of a decree (38)

Above the iota of line 1 there is enough vertical space for one more line to have been inscribed, but there is no trace of inscription here, suggesting that this fragment derives from the prescript of a decree.

Line 2: The top of the vertical and the beginning of the loop of rho survive.

Line 3: The second vertical of pi is partly preserved in the break.

Line 4: The apex of alpha and the upper third of nu survive.

Tracy attributes this document to the "Cutter of *IG* II² 495," who, so far, appears to have worked only during the years of ca. 304/3 to ca. 303/2 B.C.[45]

Line 1: [Ἐρεχθ]είδ[ος], [Αἰγ]είδ[ος], or [Οἰν]είδ[ος].

Its thickness indicates that this stele was probably very wide.[46]

39 Fragment of a decree Fig. 39

I 2581. A fragment of a stele of pale blue Hymettian marble discovered on March 15, 1935, southwest of the Tholos (F 12), in a mixed Classical to Late Roman context. It is broken all around and on the back. The face still bears horizontal and diagonal marks of the finishing rasp. Tracy published this fragment in 2003.[47]

H. 0.064, W. 0.108, Th. 0.02; L.H. 0.006–0.007; stoich. hor. 0.0125, vert. 0.014.

End of 4th century B.C. Stoich.

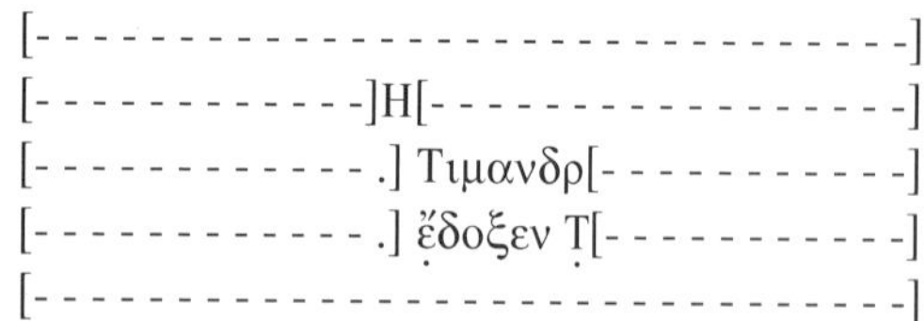

[- -]
[- - - - - - - - - - - -]Η[- - - - - - - - - - - - - - - - -]
[- - - - - - - - - - - - .] Τιμανδρ[- - - - - - - - - - -]
[- - - - - - - - - - - - .] ἔ̣δοξεν Τ̣[- - - - - - - - - - -]
[- -]

Line 1: The bottom of the right vertical and part of the horizontal of an eta are visible. Tracy prints a dotted nu.

Line 2: The faint triangular letter visible in the photograph at the right edge is too close to the rho and is merely a product of the finishing rasp; however, the

44. See n. 40, above.

45. *ADT,* pp. 160–163; description of the lettering of *IG* II² 495, pp. 161–162; photograph, p. 161, fig. 17.

46. According to "Dow's Formula," in which the ratio of thickness:width: height is 1:4½:9; see Dow 1942.

47. *AAM,* pp. 104–107, no. 1; photograph, p. 106, fig. 37.

Figure 39. Fragment of a decree (39)

left third of this stoichos survives uninscribed, which suggests that a letter such as iota was inscribed here, not an omicron.

Line 3: The tip of the topmost horizontal of epsilon is visible before delta. The left tip of the horizontal of a tau is preserved after nu. Tracy does not print this letter.

The shapes of alpha, epsilon, mu, nu, omicron, and rho seem characteristic of the work of the "Cutter of *IG* II² 495."[48] Tracy attributes this fragment to the "Cutter of Agora I 6664," however, active between 281/80 and ca. 240 B.C.[49]

Line 2: Τιμανδρ[ίδης], or more likely, Τιμανδρ[ίδου]?
Line 3: ἔ̣δοξεν τ̣[(ῆι βουλῆι καὶ τ)ῶι δήμωι]?

40 Fragment of a decree — Fig. 40

I 6324. A fragment of a stele of micaceous Pentelic marble discovered on April 4, 1951, east of the Altar of Ares (M 8), in a Late Roman context. The polished left side is preserved, with a margin of 0.012.

H. 0.06, W. 0.092, Th. 0.045; L.H. 0.006–0.007; non-stoich. vert. 0.013.

Figure 40. Fragment of a decree (40)

End of 4th century B.C. — Non-stoich.

[- -]

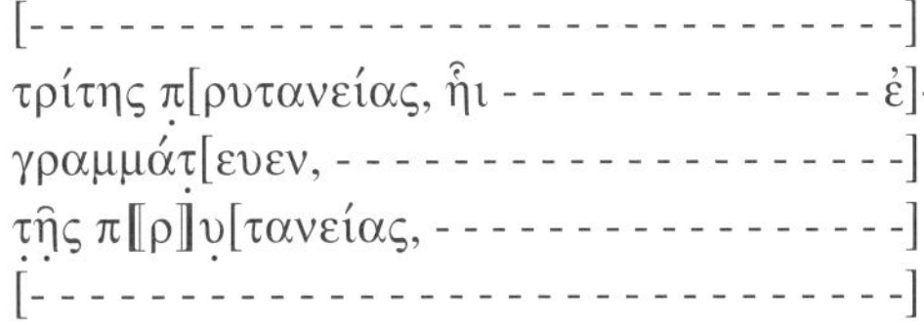
τρίτης π̣[ρυτανείας, ἧι - - - - - - - - - - - - - ἐ]-
γραμμάτ̣[ευεν, -]
τ̣ῆ̣ς π⟦ρ⟧υ̣[τανείας, - - - - - - - - - - - - - - - - -]
[- -]

Line 1: The first vertical and most of the horizontal of pi survive.

Line 2: The left tip of the bar of tau survives on the break.

Line 3: Despite the abraded surface, the bar of the tau is partly preserved, but most of the eta has disappeared. In the fifth stoichos the mason tried unsuccessfully to correct an error: the loop of rho is attached to the second vertical of the eta that was originally cut here. The top of the left diagonal of upsilon survives after this.

Above line 1 it is probable that an archon formula and the first half of a prytany formula were inscribed, [ἐπὶ - - - - ἄρχοντος, ἐπὶ τῆς - - - -].

The line length will have been between ca. 32 and ca. 43 letters, depending upon the lengths of the archon's and the prytany's names.

41 Fragment of a decree conferring citizenship upon certain Prienians — Fig. 41

I 5492. A fragment of a stele of micaceous Pentelic marble discovered on June 1, 1938, below course 4 of the west wall of the Klepsydra

48. See n. 45, above.
49. *AAM*, pp. 99–111; description of lettering, pp. 99–101; photograph of Agora I 6664 (squeeze), p. 100, fig. 31.

Figure 41. Fragment of a decree conferring citizenship upon certain Prienians (41)

antechamber (T 27:1), in a Classical context. It is broken all around and on the back. It is part of, but does not join, *IG* II[2] 566 (EM 7325), corresponding to lines 12–15 of that decree.

H. 0.052, W. 0.084, Th. 0.07; L.H. 0.005; non-stoich. vert. 0.012.

End of 4th century B.C. Non-stoich. ca. 52?

[προεδρ]-
ύειν εἰς τὴν πρώτην ἐκκλησ[ίαν τὴν μετὰ τὸν . .]Α̣Ι̣ΕΝΑ̣[. . . ca. 10 . . .]
ον γιγνομένην προσαγαγε[ῖν τοὺς τῶν Πριηνέ]ων ΚΑΤΑ̣[. . . ca. 10 . . .]
χρηματίσαι ὑπὲρ τῆς δωρεᾶ[ς αὐτοῖς· γνώμην] δὲ ξυμβ̣[άλλεσθαι τῆς]
βουλῆς εἰς τὸν δῆμον ὅτι [. . . . . ca. 15 . . . . .]Μ̣ΕΝΘΗ̣[. . . ca. 10 . . ., Μα]-
καρέα Λυκωπάδου, Θ[- -]

The text of the new fragment is underlined.

Line 12 (= line 1 of I 5492): In the first and second stoichoi the base of a right diagonal is followed by that of a central vertical; in the fifth stoichos the base of a left diagonal is visible.

Line 13: The base of the left diagonal of alpha survives at the right edge.

Line 14: The upper left corner of beta is preserved.

Line 15: The right apex of mu survives in the first stoichos; in the fifth the top of a left vertical is preserved.

Line 13: κατα̣[γγέλους κα̣ὶ]?

Line 15: ὅτι [δοκεῖ <τεῖ βουλεῖ>, ἐπαινέσαι] μ̣ὲν Θη̣[- - - -]?

42 Fragment from the conclusion of an honorific decree Fig. 42

I 4896. A fragment of a stele of pale gray Hymettian marble discovered on May 18, 1937, on the north slope of the Acropolis (T 26), on the surface. It is broken all around and on the back. Traces of two carved wreaths survive below the last inscribed line.

H. 0.129, W. 0.118, Th. 0.045; L.H. 0.008; stoich. 0.016 (square).

End of 4th century B.C. Stoich.

[- -]
[- - - - - - - - - - . . . .]ΣΤ[- - - - - - - - - - - -]
[- - - - - - - - - πρά]ττει κ[αὶ - - - - - - - - -]
[- - - - - - - - - . Ἀ]θήναζε [- - - - - - - - - -]
wreath *wreath*

Figure 42. Fragment from the conclusion of an honorific decree (42)

The language suggests a context similar to that of *IG* II[2] 484 + 558, of 304/3 B.C., by which the honorand was rewarded for his past activities in the expectation of his performing further services, namely the retrieval and return to Athens of war captives.[50]

43 Fragment of an honorific decree — Fig. 43

I 4491. A fragment of a stele of slightly micaceous Pentelic marble found on February 2, 1937, on the north slope of the Areopagus (L–N 18–20), in a pile of marble. The smooth-dressed left side is preserved. The stone is very badly abraded, with patches of mortar adhering to its surface.

H. 0.22, W. 0.153, Th. 0.08; L.H. 0.006; stoich. hor. 0.0105, vert. 0.0095.

End of 4th century B.C. — Stoich.

[- -]
[. . . . . .¹³. . . . . .]Ι̣[- - - - - - - - - - - - - - - - - - -]
[. . . . . .¹³. . . . . .]Λ̣[- - - - - - - - - - - - - - - - - - -]
[. .]σ̣τ̣εφ[α]ν[- -]
[.]ς ἕνεκα κ[αὶ εὐ]νοί̣[ας τῆς - - - - - - - - - - - -]
[. .]Ι̣ δὲ αὐτ[οῦ κα]ὶ Ε[- - - - - - - - - - - - - - - - -]
[ι] π̣λὴν [.]Α̣Ρ̣Α̣[- - - - - - - - - - - - - - - - - - - -]
[τ]ῆς εἰκό[ν]ο[ς -]
[. . .]ΝΗΟ[- -]
[. . .]ΑΥΠΟ̣[- -]
[.]Ε̣ΣΘΑΙ[- -]
[.] δὲ τῶι δ̣[ήμ]ω̣[ι - - - - - - - - - - - - - - - - - - -]
[.] καὶ ΤΑΥ[- -]
[.]ΚΟΘΩΝΝ[- -]
[.]ΤΟΚΕΙ[- -]
[.]Λ̣ΙΛ̣[- -]
[. .]ΜΜ̣Α̣[- -]
[. . .]Λ̣[.]Λ̣[- -]
[- - - - - - - - - - - - *traces* - - - - - - - - - - - - - - - - -]
[- - - - - - - - - - - - *traces* - - - - - - - - - - - - - - - - -]
[- - - - - - - - - - - - *traces* - - - - - - - - - - - - - - - - -]

Lines 1 and 2: In line with the omicron of line 4, the outlines of a central vertical and, below it, those of a triangular letter, can be seen.

Line 3: The lowest diagonal of sigma, then the base of a central vertical, the lower half of the vertical and the two lowest horizontals of epsilon, and the bottom of the vertical and of the loop of phi, survive; the lower right corner of nu is visible in the sixth stoichos.

Line 4: The faint outlines of alpha and the second kappa are visible; at the right edge the lower part of nu, most of the omicron, and the upper part of iota can be seen.

Line 5: The bottom of iota survives, followed a faint delta. The outlines of iota and epsilon survive below the nu and omicron of line 4.

Line 6: Both verticals of pi survive, but not its horizontal. In the seventh and ninth stoichoi the diagonals of two alphas are visible and, between the alphas, the vertical and the beginning of the loop of rho.

50. For the date, see n. 40, above.

Figure 43. Fragment of an honorific decree (43)

Line 9: The upper curve of omicron is preserved.

Line 11: The apex of the second delta survives; two spaces to the right of this a circular depression are probably the remains of an omega.

Line 13: The diagonals of kappa and the outlines of omicron and theta survive before the omega. The shape of omega seems quite different from that of the first omega in line 11; it may represent the correction of a mistake.

Line 15: The apices of two triangular leters are visible, a central vertical between them.

Line 16: The right apex of mu, a second mu, and the apex of alpha survive.

Line 17: The apices of two triangular letters are visible.

Lines 18–20: There are traces of letters here, but too worn and too faint to provide secure readings.

The hand is unfamiliar, but seems characteristic of the late 4th or early 3rd century B.C.

Line 3: The award of a crown: στεφ[α]ν[ῶσαι]? Probably of gold.

Lines 4–5: [ἀρετ|ῆ]ς ἕνεκα κ[αὶ εὐ]νοί̣[ας τῆς πρὸς τὸν δῆμον τὸν Ἀθηναίων]?

Lines 4–6: [στῆ|σα]ι̣ δὲ αὐτ[οῦ κα]ὶ ε[ἰκόνα χαλκῆν ἐν ἀγορᾶι ὅπου ἂν βούληται|ι] π̣λὴν [π]α̣ρ̣' Ἀ̣[ρμόδιον καὶ Ἀριστογείτονα]? These restorations require a line of 46 letters.[51]

The context may be the "liberation" of Athens by Demetrios Poliorketes in 307/6 B.C., but a later date is not out of the question.

51. For the formulas used in honorary inscriptions, see Henry 1983, pp. 294–300.

44 Fragment of a decree honoring the councillors from Pandionis — Fig. 44

I 6246. A fragment of a stele of Pentelic marble discovered on October 22, 1949, between the east end of the Middle Stoa and the Stoa of Attalos (P 12), in a late context. It is broken all around and on the back. There is a vertical uninscribed space of 0.03 below the last line.

H. 0.12, W. 0.075, Th. 0.08; L.H. 0.008 (line 1), 0.006 (lines 2–9); stoich. 0.011 (square).

End of 4th century B.C. — Stoich. ca. 73–87?

[- Θε]ο̣[ί -]
[- - - - - - - - - - - - - - - - . . . .9. . . . καὶ αὐτὸ]ς̣ συνεπ[ιμεμέληται θυσιάζων πάσας τὰς θυσίας -]
[- - - - - - - - - - - - - - - - . . .5. . ἔθυσεν δὲ καὶ] ἐκ τῶν [ἰδίων -]
[- - - - ἐπαινέσαι δὲ τοὺς πρυτάνεις τῆς Πα]νδιονίδ̣[ος καὶ στεφανῶσαι (χρυσῶι στεφάνωι?) κατὰ τὸν νόμον σπουδῆς]
[ἕνεκα καὶ φιλοτιμίας τῆς πρὸς τὴν βουλὴ]ν καὶ τὸ[ν δῆμον τὸν Ἀθηναίων - - - - - - - - - - - - - -]
[- -] εἰσίν *v* [- - - - - - - - - - - - - - - - *vacat*? - - - - - - - - - -]
vacat

Line 1: The bottom of a circular letter survives, both larger than, and set above and between, the nu and epsilon of line 2.

Line 2: The tip of the lower diagonal of the first sigma is visible; at the right edge the stone breaks on the first vertical of pi.

The hand, spacing, and marble are the same as those of *Agora* XVI, no. 111 (Woodhead 1960, no. 157 + *IG* II^2 564 [I 5295 + EM 7157]), dated between 307/6 and 302/1 B.C.[52] This provides an approximate date for this fragment.

Line 2: A partial model for this restoration is *Agora* XV, no. 85, line 14.

Line 3: Cf. *Agora* XV, no. 85, line 15.

Line 4: Cf. *Agora* XV, no. 86, lines 1–2.

Line 5: Cf. *Agora* XV, no. 86, lines 2–3.

Line 6: [ἀναγεγραμμένοι] εἰσίν? Cf. *IG* II^2 643, line 9.

Figure 44. Fragment of a decree honoring the councillors from Pandionis (44)

52. Photographs of the fragments of *Agora* XVI, no. 111: Woodhead 1960, pl. 26 (= I 5295); and Pečírka 1966, pl. 16 (*IG* II^2 564 = EM 7157).

45 Fragment of a proxeny decree Fig. 45

I 3793. A fragment of a stele of very micaceous Pentelic marble discovered on March 18, 1936, west of the Odeion (J 11), in a late context. It is broken all around and on the back.

H. 0.128, W. 0.051, Th. 0.085; L.H. 0.004–0.005; stoich. hor. 0.0093, vert. 0.01 (almost square).

End of 4th century B.C.? Stoich. 35 (36)

[- -]
[. . .6. . .]HΛ̣[. . . . . .25. . . . . πε]-
[ρὶ τὸν δ]ῆ̣μον [τὸν Ἀθηναίων· εἶναι δὲ αὐτοὺς π]-
[ροξένο]υ̣ς κ[αὶ εὐεργέτας· ἐπιμελεῖσθαι δὲ α]-
[ὐτῶν τὴ]ν̣ βο[υλὴν τὴν ἀεὶ βουλεύουσαν καὶ τοὺ]- (36)
[ς στρατ]ηγοὺ[ς ὅπως ἂν μηδ᾽ ὑφ᾽ ἑνὸς ἀδικῶνται]
[ἀναγρά]ψαι δ̣[ὲ τόδε τὸ ψήφισμα ἐν στήληι λιθί]- (36)
[νηι τὸν] γραμ[ματέα τῆς βουλῆς καὶ στῆσαι ἐν ἀ]- (36)
[κροπόλ]ει· εἰ[ς δὲ τὴν ἀναγράφην καὶ ποίησιν]
[τῆς στήλ]ης [δοῦναι κτλ. - - - - - - - - - - - - -]

Line 1: The bases of the verticals and the bar of eta and the base of the left diagonal of lambda are preserved.

Line 2: The top of the right hasta of eta survives.

Line 3: The tip of the right diagonal of upsilon is preserved.

Line 4: The lower right corner of nu survives.

Line 9: The tops of the verticals and part of the bar of eta are preserved.

The hand, letter sizes, and horizontal spacing seem identical to those of *Agora* XVI, no. 111. This provides an approximate date for this fragment.[53]

The line length varies between 35 and 36 letters.

Lines 2–3: For the restoration, cf. *IG* II[2] 252, lines 9–12.

Lines 3–5: For the restoration, cf. *IG* II[2] 77, etc.

Figure 45. Fragment of a proxeny decree (45)

46 Fragment of a decree Fig. 46

I 3858. The upper right corner of a pedimental stele of heavily weathered, pale gray Hymettian marble, streaked with vertical blue lines, discovered on March 28, 1936, north of the Eleusinion (T 17), in a Byzantine pit below the floor of the Church of Christ. The right side is preserved below a projecting molding and akroterion. There is a vertical uninscribed space of 0.007 above the first line.

H. 0.111 (molding 0.01, pediment 0.045), W. 0.098, Th. 0.045 (projection of pediment 0.01); L.H. 0.005; stoich. hor. 0.01, vert. 0.011 (almost square).

End of 4th century B.C.? Stoich.

[- - - - - - - - -]ỊṆEỊΔ̣
[- - - - - - - - - .]ỌỴΣ[.]
[- - - - - - - - - . .]OΣΔ̣
[- - - - - - - - - . .]ΔẸX
[- - - - - - - - - - . . .]ΠΙ
[- - - - - - - - - - - - - -]

53. See n. 52, above.

Figure 46. Fragment of a decree (46)

Line 1: The surface is much abraded, but traces of letters survive: the top of a central vertical, the upper left corner of nu, the vertical and the upper two horizontals of epsilon, the top of iota, and the apex of delta.

Line 2: A circular depression is followed by the tops of the diagonals of upsilon, and then by the lowest diagonal of sigma; nothing survives in the final stoichos.

Line 3: Omicron is represented by a circular depression and is followed by sigma, and then by a triangular depression.

Line 4: In the first stoichos the outline of a triangular letter is preserved, but the base and interior have disappeared, so that this could be a lambda, delta, or alpha. Chi is damaged at top and bottom, so that it looks in some lights, and especially in the photograph, as if it were a badly shaped sigma.

The hand is appropriate to the end of the 4th or the beginning of the 3rd century.

Line 1: [ἐπὶ τῆς Ο]ἰ̣ν̣εί̣δ̣|[ος - - - πρυτανείας] or [ἔδοξεν τῆι Ο]ἰ̣ν̣εί̣δ̣|[ι φυλῆι]? If this is part of a decree, it will derive from the prescript, perhaps of a phyle decree.

47 Fragment of a decree — Fig. 47

I 6582. A fragment of a stele of Hymettian marble discovered on March 7, 1953, over the eastern part of the South Stoa I (N 16), in a late wall. It is broken all around and on the back.

H. 0.20, W. 0.25, Th. 0.085; L.H. 0.006–0.008 (lines 1, 3–6, 8–11), 0.007–0.008 (lines 2, 7); stoich. 0.011 (loosely square).

End of 4th century B.C.? — Stoich.

[- -]
[- - - - - . . . . . 10 . . . . .]Ẹ K[- -]

[- - - - - - . . . . 9 . . . . τ]ούτωι [- -]
[- - - - - - . . . 6 . . Ἀ]λ̣εξικακ[- -]
[- - - - - - . . . 5 . .] γ̣ενομένου [- -]
[- - - - - - . . . 5 . .]ΩΝ ἐπαρξαν[- -]
[- - - - - κεφά]λαιον τῶν χ[ρημάτων? - - - - - - - - - - - - - - - -]
[- - - - - . ἔδω]κεν εἰς τὸν [- -]
[- - - - - - - . . . .]ΛΗΙ· ὅπ⟦ω⟧ς δ[ὲ ἂν - - - - - - - - - - - - - - - - - -]
[- - - - - . χρή]ματα ἐκ τῶ̣[ν -]
[- - - - - - . . . 6 . . .]Δ̣ΗΜ[- -]
[- - - - - - - . . . 7 . . .]Λ̣ΑΝ[- -]
[- -]

Line 1: The lowest horizontal of epsilon is preserved, followed by the vertical and lower diagonal of kappa.

Line 3: The base of the right diagonal of lambda survives.

Line 4: The bottom of the vertical of gamma is preserved.

Line 8: The right diagonal and apex of lambda are visible. The omega is quite unlike those of lines 2 and 6; the mason seems to have engraved alpha here first, then converted this into an omega.

Line 9: The upper curve of omega survives.

Line 10: The upper half of delta survives.

Line 11: The apex of a triangular letter is visible below the mu of line 10.

The hand is idiosyncratic and untidy, but the letter forms seem appropriate to the end of the 4th or the beginning of the 3rd century B.C. (note, especially, the shape of upsilon).

Line 3: Either Apollo or Herakles Alexikakos? This may be a locational reference or it may deal with a sacrifice to this deity.[54]

Line 5: This suggests a religious context, perhaps the offering of first fruits (cf. *IG* II[2] 1215, lines 13–14).

Figure 47. Fragment of a decree (47)

54. There was a statue of Apollo Alexikakos in the Agora, in front, or in the porch, of the Temple of Apollo Patroos: see Paus. 1.3.4 (= *Agora* III, no. 111).

Figure 48. Fragment of a decree conferring citizenship (48)

48 Fragment of a decree conferring citizenship Fig. 48

I 4545. A fragment of a stele of Pentelic marble discovered on February 27, 1937, in the area of the Post-Herulian Wall, under Acropolis Street (T 24), in a late context. It is broken all around and on the back.

H. 0.092, W. 0.095, Th. 0.069; L.H. 0.007–008; stoich. hor. 0.015, vert. 0.0148 (almost square).

End of 4th century B.C.? Stoich. 36

[- -]
[φυλῆς καὶ δήμου καὶ φρατ]ρ̣ί̣α̣[ς ἧς ἂν βούλωντα]-
[ι· τοὺς δὲ πρυτάνεις δοῦν]αι π[ερὶ αὐτῶν τὴν ψῆ]-
[φον εἰς τὴν πρώτην ἐκκλη]σία[ν· ἀναγράψαι δὲ τ]-
[όδε τὸ ψήφισμα τὸν γραμ]ματέ[α τοῦ δήμου ἐν στ]-
[ήληι λιθίνηι καὶ στῆσα]ι ἐν ἀκ[ροπόλει· εἰς δὲ]
[τὴν ἀναγράφην τῆς στήλη]ς δ̣[οῦναι κτλ. - - - - - -]

Line 1: The bases of the verticals of rho and iota and of the left diagonal of alpha survive.

Line 3: The apparent diagonal to the left of sigma is too far to the right and so must be merely a random mark.

Line 6: The apex of delta survives.

I believe that the shapes of alpha, epsilon, nu, pi, and sigma match those of *Agora* XVI, no. 107 (I 5884), dated to 307/6 B.C.[55]

Line 1: For the omission of κατὰ τὸν νόμον, cf. *IG* II^{2} 511 and 538.

Line 3: Provision for judicial scrutiny is omitted.[56]

Figure 49. Fragment of a decree (49)

49 Fragment of a decree Fig. 49

I 3433. A fragment of a stele of Pentelic marble discovered on February 21, 1936, on Kolonos Agoraios (B 9), in Hellenistic fill. The upper left corner of a pedimental stele survives, with part of the left side, but the back has been destroyed. The left margin is 0.014.

H. 0.121 (molding 0.022, pediment 0.065), W. 0.129 (projection of molding 0.011), Th. 0.067 (projection of molding and taenia 0.013); L.H. 0.009; non-stoich., horizontal spacing 0.013–0.021.

4th/3rd century B.C.? Non-stoich.?

ἐπ' ΕΥ[- - - - - ἄρχοντος? - - - -]
[- -]

I believe that the letter forms place this in the late 4th or early 3rd century B.C. Archons in this period whose names begin Εὐ[- -] are Euxenippos (305/4 B.C.) and Euktemon (299/8 B.C.).

55. Photograph of *Agora* XVI, no. 107: Pritchett and Meritt 1940, p. 8. Tracy attributes it to the "Cutter of *IG* II^{2} 1262," active between ca. 320 and ca. 296 B.C. (*ADT,* pp. 136–149; description of lettering, pp. 136, 138; photograph, p. 137; see also *AAM,* pp. 38–48).

56. For scrutiny in citizenship grants before, in, and after 303/2 B.C., see *Naturalization* III–IV, pp. 165–166, 167. Osborne suggests that scrutiny was a characteristic of democratic regimes, but that the absence of this feature between 307/6 and 303/2 B.C. was probably a consequence of the press of other business during this period, rather than of deliberate policy.

Figure 50. Fragment of an honorific decree (50)

50 Fragment of an honorific decree Fig. 50

I 6416. A fragment of a stele of Pentelic marble discovered on September 14, 1951, northeast of the Agora (H–S 14–15), in the dump used for repairs to Lekkas Street. The pick-dressed left side is preserved. Tracy published this in 2003.[57]

H. 0.095, W. 0.083, Th. 0.032; L.H. 0.007; stoich. 0.0145 (square).

4th/3rd century B.C. Stoich.

[- -]
E[- -]-
HNAỊ[- - - - - - - - - - - - - - - - - - -]
YKAIΔ[- - - - - - - - - - - - - - - - - - χ]-
ρυσῶι [στεφάνωι - - - - - - - - - - - -]
ARMIΔ[- - - - - - - - - - - - - - - - - -]
YΣKẠ[- - - - - - - - - - - - - - - - - - -]
[- -]

Line 1: The lower half of epsilon is preserved. Tracy prints a dotted iota.

Line 2: The base of iota survives at the right. Tracy dots the eta, and does not print alpha or iota.

Line 4: Tracy prints στεφάνωι without a square bracket.

Line 5: Tracy dots the alpha.

Line 6: The apex of alpha is visible. Tracy prints only the sigma.

The shapes of alpha, epsilon, kappa, mu, rho, sigma, and omega are matched in *Agora* XVI, no. 122 (I 5709), dated to 302 B.C., which is also attributed by Tracy to the "Cutter of *IG* II² 1262."[58]

Lines 1–2: [εἰς τὸν δῆμον τὸν Ἀθ]|ηναị́[ων]?

Lines 3–6: [εἶναι δὲ - - - χ]|αρμίδ[ην καὶ - - - Ἀθηναίους αὐτο]|ὺς κạ[ὶ ἐκγόνους αὐτῶν κτλ.]? Tracy suggests that this name may be either Charmides or Polycharmides.[59]

51 Fragment of an honorific decree Fig. 51

I 5771. A fragment of a stele of creamy-white Pentelic marble discovered on April 4, 1939, east of Klepsydra (U 26), in a modern context. It is broken all around and on the back.

H. 0.138, W. 0.107, Th. 0.052; L.H. 0.007; stoich. hor. 0.0126, vert. 0.0133.

57. *AAM*, pp. 38, 46–48, no. 2; photograph, p. 47, fig. 4.

58. Photograph of *Agora* XVI, no. 122: Schweigert 1940, p. 349, no. 45 (see also n. 52, above, and *ADT*, pp. 136–149).

59. *AAM*, p. 47, and n. 23.

Figure 51. Fragment of an honorific decree (51)

4th–3rd century B.C. Stoich.

[- -]
[- - - - - - - - - - . . .]ỊΤΟΙΣ[- - - - - - - - - - - - - - - - - - - -]
[- - - - - - - - -] κ̣αὶ παρὰ Ṭ[- - - - - - - - - - - - - - - - - - -]
[- - - - - - - - -]ỌΙΣΤΑΣ⟦Π⟧Ρ̣[- - - - - - - - - - - - - - - - -]
[- - - - - - - - - - .]ẸΡΙΑΙΚΑ[- - - - - - - - - - - - - - - - - - -]
[- - - - - - - - - - . .]ΕΙΚΑΙẸ[- - - - - - - - - - - - - - - - - - - -]
[- - - - - - - - - - . . .]ΥΒΑΣ[- - - - - - - - - - - - - - - - - - - -]
[- - - - - - - - - - . . .]Ṇ̣ΟΙΑ[- - - - - - - - - - - - - - - - - - - -]
[- - - - - - - - - - . . . .]ỊΛ[- -]
[- -]

Line 1: In the first stoichos the base of a central vertical survives in the break.

Line 2: The tips of both diagonals of kappa and the left tip of the horizontal of tau are visible.

Line 3: The upper right curve of a circular letter survives to the left of iota. The mason corrected a gamma to a pi by adding a very faint second vertical; to the right of this the upper left corner of rho is visible; the right part and bottom of the loop have disappeared.

Line 4: The tips of the horizontals of epsilon are visible.

Line 5: A left vertical survives in the sixth stoichos; faint horizontal marks at top and bottom suggest that this is an epsilon, rather than a gamma or pi.

Line 7: The top of the right vertical of nu survives.

The hand is appropriate to the late 4th or early 3rd century.

Line 4: [ἐλευθ]ερίαι κα[ὶ - -]?
Line 6: [το]ῦ βασ[ιλέως]?
Line 7: [εὐ]ṇοία[ς ἕνεκα (or τῆς) - -]?

What survives in lines 6–8 suggests that some friend of one of the Macedonian kings is involved; if so, a date before 301 B.C. seems likely.

52 Fragment from the conclusion of a decree Fig. 52

I 978b. A fragment of a stele of micaceous, bluish Pentelic marble discovered on January 19, 1934, between the Stoa of Zeus and the Temple of Apollo Patroos (G–K 5–8), in a marble dump. It is broken all around and on the back. There is a vertical uninscribed space of 0.052 below the last inscribed line.

H. 0.129, W. 0.033, Th. 0.045; L.H. 0.007; stoich. hor. 0.01, vert. 0.014.

4th/3rd century B.C. Stoich.

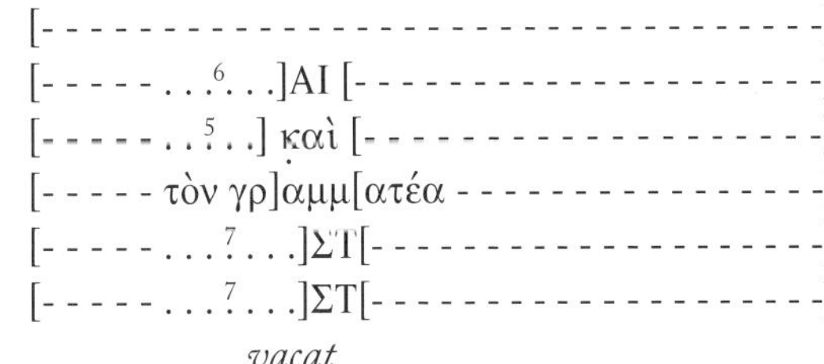

[- -]
[- - - - - . . .⁶. . .]ΑΙ [- - - - - - - - - - - - - - - - - - -]
[- - - - - . . .⁵. .] κ̣αὶ [- - - - - - - - - - - - - - - - - - -]
[- - - - - τὸν γρ]αμμ[ατέα - - - - - - - - - - - - - - - -]
[- - - - - . . .⁷. . .]ΣΤ[- - - - - - - - - - - - - - - - - - -]
[- - - - - . . .⁷. . .]ΣΤ[- - - - - - - - - - - - - - - - - - -]
vacat

Line 2: The tip of the lowest diagonal of a kappa is preserved.

The hand is appropriate to the late 4th or early 3rd century.

This probably derives from the conclusion of a decree, but no very convincing restoration comes to mind.

Figure 52. Fragment from the conclusion of a decree (52)

Figure 53. Fragment of a decree conferring citizenship (53)

53 Fragment of a decree conferring citizenship Fig. 53

I 4648. A fragment of a stele of blue-gray Hymettian marble discovered in March 27, 1937, on the north slope of the Acropolis, west of the Post-Herulian Wall (S–T 26), at the surface. It is broken all around. The rough-picked back is probably not original.

H. 0.065, W. 0.10, Th. 0.043; L.H. 0.005–0.006; non-stoich. vert. 0.0132.

4th/3rd century B.C. Non-stoich. ca. 35?

[- -]
[- - εἶναι - - -]Α̣[.]ΑΚΟΝΤ̣Α̣[- - - - - - ca. 14 - - - - - -]
[. . . Ἀθηναῖον] αὐτὸν καὶ ἐκ[γόνους αὐτοῦ καὶ]
[εἶναι αὐτῶι γρ]άψασθαι φ[υλῆς καὶ δήμου καὶ]
[φρατρίας ἧς ἂν βο]ύλη[ται κτλ. - - - - - - - - - - - -]

Line 1: The base of the right diagonal of alpha (or lambda) survives above the tau of line 2; at the right edge the bases of a vertical and of a left diagonal are visible. Note the very low position of the lower diagonal of kappa.

Line 2: The base of the vertical of the second kappa survives at the right.

Line 4: The diagonals and the top of the vertical of upsilon are preserved.

The marble, letter forms, and non-stoichedon arrangement all suggest a date for this fragment late in the 4th or early in the 3rd century B.C.

For the restorations, cf. *IG* II² 558, lines 17–21.

54 Fragment of an honorific decree Fig. 54

I 4981. A fragment of a stele of Pentelic marble discovered on June 16, 1937, over the paved court below Klepsydra (T 26–27), in the original filling of the Post-Herulian Wall. It is broken all around, but the rough-picked back may be partially preserved. The stone shows traces of burning.

H. 0.149, W. 0.13, Th. 0.115; L.H. 0.006–0.007; stoich. 0.0135 (square).

4th/3rd century B.C. Stoich.

[- -]
[- - - - - . . . 7 . . .]ΕΠ̣[- -]
[- - - - - . . . 6 . . .]ΔΑΤΙ̣[- -]
[- - - - - ἕνεκα] κ̣αὶ ε⟦ὐ⟧ν[οίας τῆς - - - - - - - - - - - - - - -]

Figure 54. Fragment of an honorific decree (54)

[- - - - - . . 5 . .]ΣΣΤΡΑṬ[- -]
[- - - - - . . 5 . .][[κ]]ράτου̣[ς - - - - - - - - - - - - - - - - - - -]
[- - - - - . . ἐπα]ι[[νέσ]]α[ι -]
[- - - - - . . . 6 . . .]ΝΑΠ[[Ο]]Ṭ[- - - - - - - - - - - - - - - - - - -]
[- - - - - . . . 6 . . .]ṆΩΠΟΥ̣[- - - - - - - - - - - - - - - - - - - -]
[- - - - - . . . 7 . . .]ΕΚΑ[- -]
[- -]

Line 1: The lower third of a left vertical is preserved after epsilon.

Line 2: The lower third of a central vertical survives at the right edge.

Line 3: The tip of the lower diagonal of kappa is visible; in the fifth stoichos the mason began to inscribe a chi, then corrected this to an upsilon.

Line 4: The lower part of the vertical of tau survives in the break.

Line 5: In the first stoichos the mason began to inscribe the horizontals of an epsilon, then corrected this to a kappa; in the sixth stoichos the tip of the left diagonal of upsilon is preserved.

Line 6: In the second, third, and fourth stoichoi the mason first inscribed kappa, sigma, and epsilon, and then corrected these to nu, epsilon, and sigma.

Line 7: In the fourth stoichos the mason began to inscribe a chi, then corrected it to an omicron; after this the left tip of the horizontal of tau survives.

Line 8: In the first stoichos the top of the right hasta of a nu survives, and in the last, so does the tip of the left diagonal of upsilon. The omega is merely a narrow oval with a slight gap at its base.

The lettering is inconsistent, with a tendency to thicken the free ends of straight strokes; the crossbar of alpha is set very high; the middle horizontal of epsilon is shorter and the vertical tends to overlap the lowest horizontal; omicron is very small and made with a series of straight strokes; rho has a tiny loop; the outer diagonals of sigma are almost flat; and omega is a small, somewhat lopsided horseshoe: these letters are distinctive, but hard to match in other inscriptions. The best comparison may be with *IG* II² 585 (= *SEG* XXI 352, EM 7068), dated to 300/299 B.C., whose letters display a similar inconsistency, and some of whose

Figure 55. Fragment of a decree (55)

alphas, epsilons, rhos, sigmas, and upsilons are identical. Its omega, however, is quite different. The inconsistency and the number of mistakes suggest that this is the work of an inexperienced mason.

The thickness of this fragment suggests that the original stele must have been unusually wide, with correspondingly long lines of text.[60]

55 Fragment of a decree Fig. 55

I 3211. A fragment of a stele of micaceous Pentelic marble discovered on September 28, 1935, northeast of the Odeion (N 8), in a modern house wall. The rough-picked back is preserved. Above the single surviving line of inscription there is a vertical uninscribed space of 0.031.

H. 0.08, W. 0.13, Th. 0.13; L.H. 0.005; stoich.? hor. 0.008.

4th/3rd century B.C. Stoich.?

[ἐπὶ - - - - -]ά̣τ̣ο̣υ̣ ἄ̣ρ̣χοντ[ος, - - - - - - - - -]
[- -]

Line 1: Traces visible in the break are the apex of alpha, the bar and upper part of the vertical of tau, the upper curve of omicron, the tips of the diagonals of upsilon, the apex of alpha, and the upper left corner of rho.

Line 1: [Λεωστρ]ά̣τ̣ο̣υ̣ (303/2 B.C.), or [Νικοστρ]ά̣τ̣ο̣υ̣ (295/4 B.C.)?

The thickness of this fragment indicates that its stele was probably very wide;[61] thus, it may be part of a prytany or ephebic decree.

56 Fragment of a proxeny decree Fig. 56

I 2835. A fragment of a stele of Pentelic marble found on April 24, 1935, over the north part of the Middle Stoa (O 13), in an Early Byzantine context. The right side is preserved.

60. According to Dow's Formula; see n. 46, above.

61. According to Dow's Formula; see n. 46, above.

Figure 56. Fragment of a proxeny decree (56)

H. 0.08, W. 0.043, Th. 0.034; L.H. 0.006; stoich. 0.013 (square).

4th/3rd century B.C. Stoich. 43

[- -]
[- εὐνοίας ἕνεκα κα]ὶ φ-
[ιλοτιμίας τῆς εἰς τὸν δῆμον τὸν Ἀθηναίων· εἶναι δ]ὲ <α>ὐ-
[τοὺς καὶ ἐκγόνους αὐτῶν καὶ προξένους καὶ εὐεργ]έτ<α>-
[ς Ἀθηναίων καὶ ἐπιμελεῖσθαι αὐτῶν τὴν βουλὴν καὶ] το-
[ὺς πρυτάνεις καὶ τοὺς στρατηγοὺς οὗ ἂν δέωνται κα]ὶ τ-
[ὴν προξενίαν αὐτοῖς ἀναγράψαι τὸν γραμματέα τὸν] κα̣-
[τὰ πρυτανείαν κτλ. -]

Line 6: The apex of alpha is preserved.

The mason has a tendency to thicken the free ends of straight letter strokes; the crossbar of alpha is omitted; the lowest horizontal of epsilon slopes down to the right and is a little longer than the upper horizontals; the diagonals of kappa are long and meet at an acute angle; and omicron is medium-sized and made by a series of short, straight cuts, so that it is more polygonal than circular, and its upper curve overlaps the lower on the left. The few surviving letters most closely resemble those of Tracy's "Cutter of *IG* II² 478," active between 305/4 and 302/1 B.C.; note the shapes of alpha, epsilon, omicron, and phi.[62]

Line 1: Award of a gold crown, either [ἀπὸ: Χ: δραχμῶν] or [κατὰ τὸν νόμον], depending on the date?[63]

57 Fragment of a decree conferring citizenship Fig. 57

I 5505. A fragment of a stele of Pentelic marble found on June 4, 1938, over the east wall of the paved court below Klepsydra (U 27), in a Roman context. It is broken on all sides and on the back. The lettering is very shallow.

H. 0.07, W. 0.088, Th. 0.045; L.H. 0.004–0.005; stoich. 0.012 (square).

4th/3rd century B.C. Stoich. 48

[- -]
[. . . . . . 13 . . . . . .]ΣΤΕ̣[. . . . . 32 . . . .]-
[. . . . . . 13 . . . . . .]ΤΙΕ<Α>Ν[. . . . . 30 . . . .]-
[. . . . 9 . . . . αὐτὸ]ν κ<α>ὶ <Ἀ>θ[ηναῖον καὶ ἐκγόνους αὐτοῦ καὶ ἐξεῖν]-
[αι αὐτῶι γράψα]σθ<α>ι [φυλῆς καὶ δήμου καὶ φρατρίας ἧς ἂν βούλ]-
[ηται κατὰ τὸν ν]ὀ̣μ̣[ον κτλ. -]

Line 1: The lowest horizontal of what may be an epsilon is visible, but the vertical has disappeared.

Line 2: The left vertical and the beginning of the diagonal of nu survive.

Line 5: The upper right curve of omicron and the left apex of mu survive.

The mason tends to make his straight letter strokes with a slight upward or outward curve; the crossbar of alpha is omitted; the vertical of epsilon overlaps the upper and lower horizontals, and the central horizontal is short and does not meet the vertical; theta (and perhaps also omicron) is small and made with two semicircles that do not quite meet at the left; the diagonals of kappa are short and the lower is nearly horizontal; the top diagonal of sigma is nearly horizontal and overlaps the second, while the third overlaps the lowest diagonal, which is also

62. *AAM,* pp. 56–61; description of letters, pp. 56–59; photographs of *IG* II² 478d and 478e (squeezes), p. 57, fig. 7, and p. 58, fig. 8.

63. See n. 40, above.

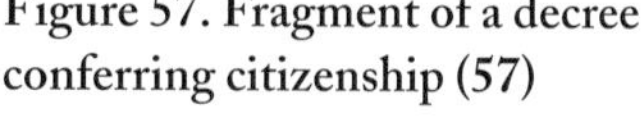

Figure 57. Fragment of a decree conferring citizenship (57)

nearly horizontal. These features, except sigma, are characteristic of *Agora* XVI, no. 152 (I 2767), and this fragment may therefore be of similar date.[64]

58 Fragment of a decree — Fig. 58

I 3293. A fragment of a stele of Pentelic marble discovered on January 28, 1936, in the area of South Stoa I and II (N–O 16–17), in a marble dump. It is broken all around. The back is flat, rough-picked, and probably reworked.

H. 0.115, W. 0.12, Th. 0.075; L.H. 0.007; stoich. hor. 0.0145, vert. 0.014 (almost square).

298/7 or 297/6 B.C.? — Stoich.

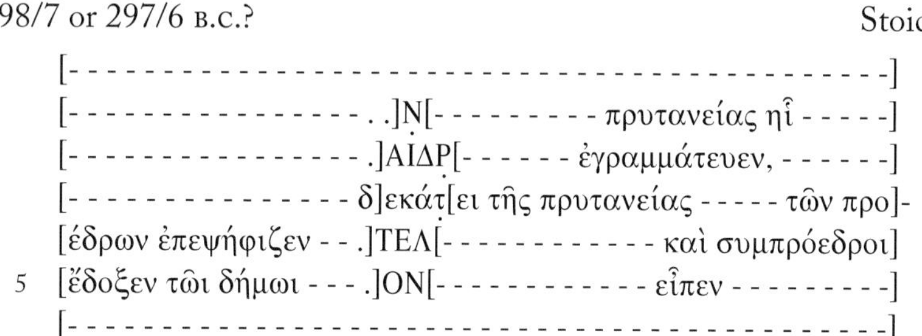

[- -]
[- - - - - - - - - - - - - - - - . .]Ṇ[- - - - - - - - - πρυτανείας ηῑ - - - - -]
[- - - - - - - - - - - - - - - - .]ΑΙ̣ΔΡ̣[- - - - - - ἐγραμμάτευεν, - - - - - -]
[- - - - - - - - - - - - - - - δ]εκάτ̣[ει τῆς πρυτανείας - - - - - τῶν προ]-
[έδρων ἐπεψήφιζεν - - .]ΤΕΛ̣[- - - - - - - - - - - - καὶ συμπρόεδροι]
[ἔδοξεν τῶι δήμωι - - - .]ΟΝ[- - - - - - - - - - - - εἶπεν - - - - - - - - -]
[- -]

Figure 58. Fragment of a decree (58)

Line 1: The base of a left vertical is preserved above the iota of line 2. A nu is by no means the only possibility here, since in this mason's work iota tends to be placed in the left part of its stoichos.

Line 2: The stone breaks at the right on the base of a left vertical.

Line 3: The base of the vertical of tau survives.

Tracy attributes this document to the "Cutter of *IG* II² 1262,"[65] active between ca. 320 and ca. 296 B.C.

Line 2: Part of the name of the secretary; in the period under consideration, in only two years, 298/7 B.C. (Phyle VIII) and 297/6 B.C. (Phyle IX), is the secretary completely unknown. Possible restorations of this name are Phaidragoras, Phaidriades, Phaidrias, and Phaidrides, but none of these is attested for Phyle VIII or IX, in the period under consideration.

64. Note Woodhead's description of the lettering of I 2767 (*Agora* XVI, p. 222), which could be applied to this stone, too. Tracy attributes I 2767 to the "Cutter of *IG* II² 330" (see n. 14, above) and places it at ca. 325 B.C., but Woodhead argues convincingly for a date at the end of the 4th century B.C. or the beginning of the 3rd.

65. See n. 55, above.

Figure 59. Fragment of an honorific decree (59)

59 Fragment of an honorific decree Fig. 59

I 5361. A fragment of a stele of Pentelic marble found March 30, 1938, southeast of the Market Square, at the west edge of the Panathenaic Way (S 18), in a Byzantine context. It is broken all around and on the back.

H. 0.105, W. 0.063, Th. 0.055; L.H. 0.006 (lines 1–5), 0.007 (line 6); stoich. hor. 0.0105, vert. 0.013.

Ca. 320–296 B.C. Stoich.

[---------------------------]
[-------...]ΔΡ[---------------]
[-------. τῶ]ν ἐν̣ [ἄστει ----------]
[------- Ἐλ]ε̣υσι[νίων ----------]
[-------..]Ω̣ΣΙΚ[--------------]
[-------..]ΑΓΩΝΟ̣[------------]
[-------...]ΤΙΑΣ[-------------]
[---------------------------]

Line 1: The lower right corner of delta and the base and lower part of the loop of rho survive. The vertical is too far to the left to be that of an iota.

Line 2: The base of the left vertical of the second nu survives.

Line 3: The tip of the lowest horizontal of epsilon is preserved.

Line 4: The tip of the right horizontal extender of omega survives at the left.

Line 5: The upper left curve of omicron is visible at the right.

Tracy attributes this document to the "Cutter of *IG* II² 1262."[66]

Line 1: Part of a name?
Line 2: [καὶ ἀνειπεῖν τὸν στέφανον Διονυσίων τε τῶ]ν ἐν̣ [ἄστει]?
Line 3: [καὶ Παναθηναίων καὶ Ἐλ]ε̣υσι[νίων]?
Line 4: [τοῖς γυμνικοῖς ἀγ]ῶ̣σι κ[αὶ - - -]?
Line 5: [τὸν] ἀγωνο̣[θέτην]?

Figure 60. Fragment of a decree (reaffirming a grant of citizenship?) (60)

60 Fragment of a decree (reaffirming a grant of citizenship?) Fig. 60

I 5491. A fragment of a stele of micaceous Pentelic marble discovered on June 1, 1938, below Course 4 of the west wall of the Klepsydra antechamber (T 27: 1), in a Classical context. It is broken all around and on the back.

H. 0.09, W. 0.07, Th. 0.042; L.H. 0.004–0.005; stoich. hor. 0.0105, vert. 0.0108 (almost square).

Ca. 320–296 B.C. Stoich.

[--------------------------------]
[-------] καὶ ΣΥ[--------------------]
[-------]ΩΠΟΣΜ[-------------------]
[ ]Ο⟦Σ⟧ΒΟΥΛ[-----------------]
[-------]ΙΤΑΜΕΝ[------------------]
[-------]Ν̣ εἶνα[ι -----------------]
[-------.]ΑΙΤΕ̣[-------------------]
[-------..]Ι̣[----------------------]
[--------------------------------]

Line 1: The crossbar of alpha is set very high; after sigma, the vertical and the join of the diagonals of upsilon survive.

Line 3: The mason corrected an epsilon to a sigma, not very successfully.

66. See n. 55, above.

Line 4: The left vertical and part of the diagonal of nu survive in the break.

Line 5: The top of the second vertical of nu (or eta) survives.

Line 6: In the first stoichos the diagonals of a triangular letter are clear; a shallow horizontal stroke, perhaps a random mark, joins the bases of these diagonals; there is also an apparent crossbar at the top, set very high. Thus I print alpha here, but the possibility remains that this letter is either a delta or a lambda. After tau, the upper left corner of epsilon is preserved.

Line 7: The top of a central vertical survives below the iota of line 6.

Tracy attributes this document to the "Cutter of *IG* II² 1262."[67]

Line 1: καὶ συ[μπρόεδροι]?

Lines 2 and 3: In each line, parts of a name and patronymic?

Line 6: If the first preserved letter is, in fact, a lambda, perhaps [πο]⟦λ⟧ιτε̣[ίαν]?

61 Fragment of an honorific decree — Fig. 61

I 4530. A fragment of a stele of Pentelic marble found on February 25, 1937, southeast of the Market Square and east of the Post-Herulian Wall (T–U 22), in a Byzantine context. It is broken all around and on the back.

H. 0.045, W. 0.092, Th. 0.075; L.H. 0.006; stoich. 0.011 (square).

Ca. 320–296 B.C.? — Stoich.

[- -]
[- - - - - - - - - - - - - . .]ΚΑ̣Τ̣Α̣[- - - - - - - - - - - - - - - - - - - -]
[- - - - - - - - - - - - -]ΔΟΙΣΚ[- -]
[- - - - - - - - - - - - - .]ΠΡΟΕ̣[- -]
[- -]

Line 1: The base of the vertical and the lower diagonal of kappa survive, followed by the bases of the diagonals of both alphas and, between them, the lower part of the vertical of tau.

Line 3: The upper left corner of epsilon survives.

The shapes of kappa, pi, and sigma, and the way in which omicron is made with a series of short, straight strokes, suggest that the hand may be that of the "Cutter of *IG* II² 1262."[68]

Line 1: κα̣τ̣ὰ̣ [τὸν νόμον]? Perhaps a reference to the law regarding golden crowns.[69]

Line 2: [τραγωι]δοῖς κ[αὶ]?

Line 3: [καὶ] προε̣[δρίαν ἐν ἅπασιν τοῖς ἀγῶσιν]?[70]

Figure 61. Fragment of an honorific decree (61)

67. See n. 55, above.

68. See n. 55, above.

69. If so, in or after 304/3 B.C.; see n. 40, above.

70. See Henry 1983, pp. 291–292.

Figure 62. Fragment of a decree (reaffirming a grant of citizenship?) (62)

62 Fragment of a decree (reaffirming a grant of citizenship?) Fig. 62

I 4968. A fragment of a stele of bluish, micaceous Pentelic marble discovered on June 12, 1937, in the area west of the north part of the Stoa of Attalos (N–P 7–12), in a marble pile. The pick-dressed left side and flat, rough-picked back are preserved; the left side is slightly concave at the top; the left margin is 0.006. Marks of the finishing rasp survive on the face, from top right to bottom left.

H. 0.142, W. 0.083, Th. 0.084; L.H. 0.005; stoich. hor. 0.011, vert. 0.0108 (almost square).

Ca. 320–296 B.C.? Stoich.

[- -]
κρατης [- -]
της Ἀρ⟦χιν⟧[- -]
ΕΑΙ Θεοδ[- Ο]-
ἰνοβίου [- -]
Ι⟦ΣΙ⟧ · ἔδ[οξεν τηῖ βουλῆι καὶ τωῖ δήμωι - - - - - -]
Σ Εὐθυ[- - - - - - - - - - - - - - εἶπεν · - - - - - - - - - - -]
πατὴρ [- -]
ΕΡΟΥΗΡ[- -ἐ̣]-
⟦ν⟧ τωῖ ⟦π⟧ρ[όσθεν χρόνωι - - - - - - - - - - - - - - -]
⟦Δ⟧ΙΤΕΙ⟦Λ̣⟧[- -]
ΛΕΩΣΤ̣[- -]
[- -]

Line 2: The mason omitted chi, then corrected this mistake by erasing the iota and carving chi in its place, and replacing the nu by iota and nu, which now occupy the same stoichos.

Line 5: In the second and third stoichoi, epsilon and upsilon were corrected to sigma and iota.

Line 9: Nu is complete, but has been cut over a kappa. Similarly pi has been carved over a rho.

Line 10: In the first stoichos the first letter is apparently a delta, but has a high, angled base, quite unlike those of the deltas in lines 3 and 5; thus it may really be a lambda, the result of clumsy correction of a mistake. In the sixth stoichos the apex of a triangular letter survives, amid traces that suggest successive corrections: both a nu and an epsilon or pi were carved here, before or after the alpha, delta, or lambda was inscribed.

Line 11: The left tip of the horizontal of tau survives.

The shapes of the uncorrected letters alpha, epsilon, theta, kappa, nu, pi, rho, sigma, upsilon, and omega resemble those of the "Cutter of *IG* II² 1262."[71] The high number of errors suggests that this may be the work of a pupil in that workshop.

Line 1: The name Krates, or a compound of this?

Lines 2–3: [Εἰτ]|εαῖ(ος)?

Lines 3–4: There is no other known Attic name ending [- -]ινόβιος.[72]

Lines 4–5: In light of the correction noted above, these letters likely represent the abbreviated demotic [Κηφ]|ισι(εύς)?

Line 10: The intention may have been to inscribe some form of the word πολιτεία.

The first four lines contain the end of a list of names with patronymics and demotics; if lines 5 and 6 mark the end of the prescript of a decree, these names are probably those of a board of *symproedroi*.[73]

63 Fragments of a decree (of the Phyle Antigonis?) Fig. 63

Figure 63 *(opposite)*. Fragments of a decree (of the Phyle Antigonis?) (63): (a) fr. *a*, I 2266; (b) fr. *b*, I 5069

I 2266, I 5069. Two fragments of a stele of pale gray, white-flecked Hymettian marble found at different times and places. There is no join between the fragments. The difference in thickness between the two fragments is not a bar to their association, since it is quite usual for the backs of such stelai to be convex rather than flat.

Fragment *a* (I 2266) was discovered on December 29, 1934, over the East Building (O 14), in a modern house wall. The rough-picked back is preserved. Above the inscribed face, part of an ovolo molding survives. There is a vertical uninscribed space of 0.013 above line 1.

H. 0.115 (molding and pediment 0.042), W. 0.15, Th. 0.11.

Fragment *b* (I 5069) was discovered on November 3, 1937, south of the Market Square (O 21), in a modern house wall. Above the inscribed face the spring of a crowning molding survives. The back is flat and rough-picked, but may not be original. Part of the right side is preserved, below the surface of the face, 0.035 to the right of the upsilon of line 2. There is a vertical uninscribed space of 0.013 above line 1. This fragment was published in 2003 by Tracy.[74] He reads rather less than I do on this fragment, and differs from me in his interpretation of lines 3 and 5. There is a vertical uninscribed space of 0.013 above line 1.

H. 0.128 (molding 0.025), W. 0.08, Th. 0.085.

Both fragments: L.H. 0.005; stoich. 0.012 (square).

71. See n. 55, above.

72. Oinobios is well attested for several demes in Attica; see *LGPN* II, p. 349.

73. See n. 18, above. Whatever the demotics may be, they do not seem to be in the official order of phylai, nor are there any other surviving examples of lists of *symproedroi* who are identified by both patronymics and abbreviated demotics.

74. *AAM*, pp. 38 and 45–46, no. 1, photograph, p. 46, fig. 3.

a

b

Beginning of 3rd century B.C. Stoich.

a *b*

[- - - - - - - -]Γ̣ΟΝ[- - - - - - - - - - -]ΜΟΥΕΙ̣[. . .]
[- - - - - - - - - .]Ι̣[- - - - - - - - - - - - - .]Θ̣ΕΙΣΥ[. . .]
[- . .]ΚΑΙ[. . .]
[- .]Γ̣ΕΛ[. . . .]
[- .]Ε̣Α̣Ι̣[. . .]
[- . .]Η̣Γ̣[. . . .]
[- -]

Fragment *a,* line 1: The right tip of the horizontal and perhaps a trace of the base of the vertical of gamma survive.

Fragment *b,* line 1: The bottom of a central vertical survives at the right edge; Tracy reads Ο̣ΥΕ.

Fragment *a,* line 2: The top of a central vertical is visible below the omicron of line 1.

Fragment *b,* line 2: The first preserved letter could be either an omicron or a theta. The last preserved letter seems definitely to be an upsilon, although its lower half is not visible; Tracy prints only the epsilon.

Fragment *b,* line 3: The surface, though heavily worn, appears to be original; very faint impressions of these letters survive. Tracy describes these letters as "illegible traces."

Fragment *b,* line 4: Only the right side of the first letter survives, so that it could be either gamma or tau. Tracy prints a dotted tau and an epsilon.

Fragment *b,* line 5: The right tip of the upper horizontal of epsilon survives; the apex of alpha is preserved after epsilon, followed by the top of a central vertical. Instead of sigma, Tracy prints only a dotted upsilon.

Fragment *b,* line 6: The tops of the two verticals of eta survive, followed by the upper left corner of a rectangular letter. Tracy does not print this line.

The lettering seems appropriate to the beginning of the 3rd century B.C.; Tracy attributes fragment *b* to the "Cutter of *IG* II² 1262," using the shape of the epsilons of lines 2 and 4 as the criterion for this attribution; he may well be correct, but too few letters are preserved for certainty.

Line 1: [ἔδοξεν τῆι Ἀντι]γ̣ον[ίδι φυλῆι - - - - - -]μου Εἰ̣[τεαῖlος εἶπεν]?

Line 2: [αἱρε]θ̣εὶς (or [καταστα]θ̣εὶς, or [χειροτονη]θ̣εὶς) ὑ[πὸ - -]? Cf. *IG* II² 1157, 1158, 1159.

Line 4: [ἐπαγ]γ̣έλ[λει]?

Line 5: [ἐπαιν]έ̣σα̣ι?

64 Fragment of a decree Fig. 64

I 5049. A fragment of a stele of pale, blue-gray and white-flecked Hymettian marble from the top of a pedimental stele, discovered on October 9, 1937, south of the Market Square (P 21), in a modern house wall. The apex of the pediment survives, above a horizontal taenia, cavetto molding, and ovolo crowning molding.

H. 0.185 (molding 0.015, taenia 0.03, pediment 0.12), W. 0.21, Th. 0.096 (projection of taenia 0.015); L.H. 0.009 (line 1), 0.006–0.007 (line 2); stoich.? hor. 0.012.

Beginning of 3rd century B.C. Stoich.? ca. 29–30

[Θ]εο[ί]
[ἐπὶ - - - - - ca. 10 - - - - -]υ̣ ἄρχ̣[οντος, ἐπὶ τῆς - -]-

Figure 64. Fragment of a decree (64)

[- - - - - - - - - πρυτανείας, - - - - - - - - - - - -]
[- -]

Line 1: The two surviving letters of the invocation occupy 0.123; thus, assuming that the invocation occupied the entire width of the taenia, the stele itself will have been approximately 0.35 in width, which, in turn, allows a line length of ca. 29–30 letters.

Line 2: The tip of the right diagonal of upsilon and the upper left tip of the diagonal of chi survive.

The lettering appears appropriate to the first decade or two of the 3rd century B.C.

Line 2: [Νικοστράτο]ụ (295/4 B.C.), or [Ἀριστονύμο]ụ (289/8 B.C.)?

65 Fragment from the conclusion of a decree, followed by a list of names of members of the Phyle Leontis — Fig. 65

I 1086. A fragment of a stele of micaceous, green-veined Pentelic marble discovered on January 2, 1934, southeast of the Stoa of Zeus, in a marble pile. It is broken all around and on the back. Remains of iron attachments on the sides and face are probably modern.

H. 0.187, W. 0.075, Th. 0.055; L.H. 0.005–0.006 (lines 1–5, 7–10, 11), 0.007 (lines 6, 11); stoich. hor. 0.011, vert. 0.013 (lines 1–5), vert. 0.012 (lines 6–12). There is a slightly greater gap between lines 5 and 6 and lines 10 and 11 than between other lines.

Beginning of 3rd century B.C. — Stoich.

[- -]
[- - - - - - - . . . .⁸. . . .]ON[- - - - - - - - - - - - - - - - -]

[- - - - - - - - . . . .8. . . .]ΛΙΘ[- - - - - - - - - - - - - - - - -]
[- - - - - - - . . .7. . .]ΠΟΛΛ[- - - - - - - - - - - - - - - -]
[- - - - - - ἀναγράφ]ην τ[ῆ]ς [στήλης - - - - - - - -]
[- - - - - - - . .5. . τ]ὸ ⟦γ⟧ενό[μενον ἀνάλωμα - - -]
[- - - - - - - . . .6. . .] Σκαμβ[ωνίδαι - - - - - - - - - - -]
[- - - - - - - . .5. .]ΡΟΣΘΟΥ[- - - - - - - - - - - - - - - -]
[- - - - - - - . .5. .]Ο[.]ΗΣΜΙ[- - - - - - - - - - - - - - - -]
[- - - - - - - . .5. .]ΔΕ[. . .]Ι[- - - - - - - - - - - - - - - -]
[- - - - - - - . .5. .]ΤΟΝΟ[.]Ν[- - - - - - - - - - - - - - -]
[- - - - - - - . .5. .]^{v} Κρ⟦ω⟧π̣[ίδαι - - - - - - - - - - - - -]
[- - - - - - - . . .7. . .]ΟΜ[- - - - - - - - - - - - - - - - - -]
[- -]

Line 5: In the second stoichos the mason first inscribed a tau, then converted this to a gamma by attaching a deep vertical stroke to the left tip of the horizontal, without erasing the original vertical.

Line 6: Except for kappa, the surviving letters are very faint; after mu a deep diagonal scratch obscures most of the beta, except for part of the lower loop.

Line 9: In the second stoichos the right tips of the horizontals of epsilon survive.

Line 11: The first stoichos appears to be uninscribed; in the second the bottoms of the vertical and the lower diagonal of kappa are visible, and in the third the upper third of rho survives, followed by a very large and untidy omega, perhaps a correction, since it is more deeply cut than the other letters in this line; after this the first vertical and part of the horizontal of pi survive.

Line 12: The photograph suggests that after the mu two circular letters exist, but each lies to left of its stoichos; thus both are likely to be random marks, not letters.

The stoichedon pattern is unusual: the majority of examples of this pattern can be dated early in the 3rd century.

This may be part of a prytany decree, since lines 6–12 contain a list of names under the headings Skambonidai (line 6) and Kropidai (line 11), both demes belonging to the Phyle Leontis. Since both edges of the stone are lost, it is impossible to say whether this list derives from the first or a subsequent column of names.

Figure 65. Fragment from the conclusion of a decree, followed by a list of names of members of the Phyle Leontis (65)

66 Fragment of a decree Fig. 66

I 4740. The upper right corner of a stele of blue, white-flecked Hymettian marble discovered on April 15, 1937, west of the central part of the Stoa of Attalos (P 9), in Late Roman fill. The right side, crowning molding, horizontal taenia, and flat top are preserved.

H. 0.083 (molding 0.03, taenia 0.02), W. 0.082 (projection of molding and taenia 0.03), Th. 0.031 (at face 0.016); L.H. 0.006; stoich. 0.0145 (square).

Ca. 300–280 B.C. Stoich.

[ἐπὶ - - - - - - - ἄρχοντος, ἐπὶ τῆ]ς Οἰν̣-
[είδος - - - - - πρυτανείας, ηῖ - -]Υ̣ΣΙ
[- - - - ἐγραμμάτευεν, κτλ. - - - - - -]

Line 1: The deep vertical marks of the finishing rasp make it extremely difficult to see vertical letter strokes, but the first vertical and perhaps the bottom of the second vertical of nu survive as a slight thickening of the rasp marks in which they are placed; the same is true of the iota of line 2.

Figure 66. Fragment of a decree (**66**)

Line 2: The tip of the right diagonal of upsilon survives in the break at left.

The lettering appears appropriate to the first decade or two of the 3rd century. The shapes of omicron and sigma resemble those of Tracy's "Cutter of *IG* II² 478," but far too few letters survive for certainty.[75]

67 Fragment of a decree honoring the *sitonai* of 275/4 Fig. 67

I 1904. A fragment of a stele of pale gray, white-flecked Hymettian marble discovered on April 24, 1934, in a well in the southwest part of the Odeion (L 11), in a Late Roman context. The right side is preserved with a margin of 0.028. It joins the right side of *IG* II² 792 (EM 7397), corresponding to its lines 6–11. Tracy published this in 2003, with the join.[76]

H. 0.118, W. 0.065, Th. 0.054; L.H. 0.004 (lines 1–3), 0.005 (lines 6–11); stoich. hor. 0.01, vert. 0.013.

275/4 B.C. Stoich. 50

[- καὶ στε[φ]-
ανῶσαι αὐτῶν ἕ[καστον χρυσῶι στεφάνωι] κατὰ τὸν νόμον φιλοτ̣ι-
μίας ἕνεκα τῆς πρ[ὸς τὸν δῆμον· εἶναι δὲ αὐτ]οῖς καὶ προεδρ[ί]αν ἐ-
μ πᾶσι τοῖς ἀγῶσιν οἷς ἡ [πόλις τίθησιν κα]ὶ τὸν ἀρχιτέκτονα τὸ-
ν ἀεὶ καθιστάμενον κατανέμει[ν αὐτοῖς] τὴν θέαν· ἐπαινέ[σα]ι δὲ
καὶ τὸν γραμματέα αὐτῶν Χαιρέσ[τρατον κ]αὶ στεφ[α]ν[ῶσαι θα]λλο-
ῦ στεφάνωι· ἀναγράψαι δὲ τόδε τὸ ψήφ[ισμα καὶ τὰ ὀνόματα τῶν] σι̣-
τωνῶν κτλ.

The text of the new fragment is underlined.

Line 6 (= line 1 of I 1904): The base of vertical of tau survives.

Line 11: The upper halves of sigma and iota survive.

There is no change in the text as published, which is merely confirmed by this new fragment.[77]

Figure 67. Fragment of a decree honoring the *sitonai* of 275/4 (**67**)

75. See n. 62, above.

76. *AAM,* pp. 90–93, no. 3; photograph, p. 91, fig. 28.

77. It has not been possible to take the Agora fragment to the Epigraphic Museum, but I made a plasticine and plaster cast of its edge in 2002 and was able to fit this onto the edge of *IG* II² 792. It is worth noting here that *IG* II² 792 was also found in the area of the Agora, between the Church of Christ and the Church of the Hypapanti, that is, on the line of the Post-Herulian Wall, on the north side of the Eleusinion.

68 Fragment from the conclusion of a decree honoring the *taxiarchoi* of 275/4 — Fig. 68

I 3688. A fragment of a stele of micaceous Pentelic marble discovered on March 2, 1936, in front of the Odeion giants (M 7), in a previously excavated area. It is broken all around and on the back. There is a vertical uninscribed space of 0.062 below the last line. It belongs at the bottom of *Agora* XVI, no. 185 (I 15 + 96), corresponding to its lines 27–30, but without a join.[78]

H. 0.14, W. 0.072, Th. 0.04; L.H. 0.006; stoich. hor. 0.01, vert. 0.013.

275/4 B.C. — Stoich. 43

[ἀν]-
αγρά[ψαι δὲ τόδε τὸ ψ]ή̣φι̣[σμα τὸν γραμματέα τὸν κατὰ πρ]-
υ[τανείαν ἐν στήλει λ]ι<θ>ίνε[ι καὶ στῆσαι . . . . . .¹² . . . . .] (44)
[. . . . εἰς δὲ τὴν ἀναγ]ράφην τ̣[ῆς στήλης δοῦναι τοὺς ἐπὶ]
[τεῖ διοικησεῖ τὸ γε]νόμενο[ν ἀνάλωμα *vacat*]
vacat

The text of the new fragment is underlined.

Line 27 (= line 1 of I 3688): The base of the right hasta of eta and the base of iota survive.

Line 28: The dot of theta has been omitted. Since the first iota lies below the eta of line 1, the available space is insufficient for the words ἐν στήλει, unless a letter such as iota was cut inter-stoichos in this line.

Line 29: The left tip of the horizontal of tau survives.

Line 30: Since the first omicron lies below the rho of line 29, one of the iotas in this line, too, may have been cut inter-stoichos.

Lines 28–29: The restoration put forward in *Agora* XVI for the place of erection of the stele, [ἔμπροσθεν τοῦ στρατηγίου], requires 22 letters, too many for the space available. Perhaps, as in *Agora* XVI, no. 182, line 30, [πρὸς τῶι στρατη|γίωι]?

Figure 68. Fragment from the conclusion of a decree honoring the *taxiarchoi* of 275/4 (68)

69 Fragment of a decree — Fig. 69

I 4948. A fragment of Hymettian marble from the upper right corner of a pedimental stele, discovered on June 13, 1937, in the middle drain southeast of the Tholos (H 12), in a context of the 1st century B.C. The apex of the pediment survives, together with its right-hand corner and akroterion, above a horizontal taenia, cavetto molding, and ovolo crowning molding. The rough-picked back is preserved. The stone is so badly worn that the surviving letters are barely legible, except in vertical patches of relatively unworn stone near the center and at the right of the stele, where a few letters survive in each line; elsewhere, the letters are merely faint or incomplete outlines.

H. 0.253 (molding 0.02, taenia 0.02, pediment 0.098), W. 0.305, Th. 0.10; L.H. 0.005; non-stoich. vert. 0.011.

253/2 or 243/2 B.C.? — Non-stoich. ca. 35–37

[Θ ε] ο [ί]
[ἐπὶ Λυσιάδου ἄρχον]τ[ος], ἐπὶ [τῆς Οἰ]νείδ̣[ος - - -]
[πρυτανείας ἧι Ἀρισ]τόμα[χ]ο̣ς̣ [Ἀ]ρ̣ι̣[στο - - - - - - -]
[- - - - - - - - - - - - - - -] ἐγ̣ρ<α>μ̣[μάτευεν - - - - - - -]

78. Photograph of Agora I 15 + 96: Meritt 1933, pp. 156–158, no. 5. Tracy attributes this to the "Cutter of Agora I 3238 and 4169" (1973, pp. 190–192; 1988, pp. 304–311; *AAM*, pp. 80–98).

Figure 69. Fragment of a decree (69)

[- - - - - - - - - - - - - ἐν]ά̣[τ]ει τῆ̣[ς πρυτανείας· ἐκ]-
[κλησία κυρία· τῶν π]ροέδρω̣[ν ἐπεψήφιζεν - - - -]
[- - - - - - - - - - - - - - Λ]α̣μπτρ̣[εὺς καὶ συμπρό]-
[εδροι· ἔδοξεν τεῖ βουλεῖ] κ̣α̣ὶ [τῶι δήμωι· - - - - -]
[- -]

Line 1: The omicron lies above the pi of line 2.

Line 2: In the less abraded area at the right, the second vertical and part of the diagonal of nu, the epsilon, the iota, and the apex of delta are preserved.

Line 3: At the right the outline of omicron, the upper two diagonals of sigma, the loop of rho and the top of iota are visible.

Line 4: The outline of epsilon, the vertical of gamma, the outline of rho, alpha (without crossbar), and the first apex of mu survive.

Line 5: The diagonals of alpha survive at the left; at the right the top of the first vertical of eta is preserved.

Line 6: The upper curve of omega is visible.

Line 7: In the first stoichos the apex of alpha and in the last stoichos the upper left corner of rho survive.

Line 8: The tip of the upper diagonal of kappa, the apex of alpha, and the top of iota are visible in the break.

Line 1: [ἕκτης]?

Lines 2–3: For the restoration of the Secretary's name and the archon, see *IG* II^{2} 775, lines 27–28. For the date, see the most recent discussions of this archon's term.[79]

70 Fragment of a decree Fig. 70

I 2747a. A fragment of a stele of micaceous Pentelic marble discovered on April 12, 1935, east of the Odeion (N 10), in a Late Roman context. It is broken all around and on the back. The stele may have been erased and reused, since there seem to be traces of letters between lines 1 and 2 and above line 1.

H. 0.14, W. 0.058, Th. 0.031; L.H. 0.008–0.011 (line 1), 0.005–0.007 (lines 2–6); non-stoich. vert. 0.015.

Before the mid-3rd century B.C. Non-stoich.

[- - - - - - - - - - - - - - - - -]<E>ΙΤΡΟ[- - -]
[- - - - - - - - - - - - - - - - - .]ΗΣΔΗ̣[- - - -]
[- - - - - - - - - - - - - - - - - .]ΙΔΩ[- - - - -]
[- - - - - - - - - - - - - - - - - . .]ΛΙΣ[- - - - -]
[- - - - - - - - - - - - - - - - - . .]ΕΥ[- - - - -]
[- -]

Line 1: The middle horizontal of epsilon has been omitted.

Line 2: The top of the left vertical of eta survives at the right edge.

Line 4: The right diagonal and a faint trace of the left diagonal of a triangular letter survive; the surface between these is damaged, and the photograph suggests that there is a trace of a central bar sloping down slightly to join the right diagonal. If this is a letter stroke, this letter must be an alpha. However, if it is compared with the alpha of line 3 of **71**, which is by the same hand, it is clear that this apparent crossbar is much too high; thus, this letter is a lambda.

Figure 70. Fragment of a decree (70)

Line 1: [Δι]<ε>ιτρό[φου]?[80] Part of a heading of some sort, perhaps similar to that found in *IG* II^{2} 650 and 651, which are of approximately the same date.

Lines 2–3: [ἐπὶ τ]ῆς Δη̣[μητρι|άδος - - - πρυτανείας]?

Lines 3–4: [ῆ]ι Δω[- - - - - - - ἐγρ|αμμάτευεν]?

Line 4: [Προβα]λίσ[ιος]?

Line 5: [δ]ευ[τέραι]?

The three erased lines above and below line 1 may be read as follows:

[- - - - - - - - - - - - - - - .]Α̣[- - - - - - - - - - - - - - - - - -] [*in rasura*]
[- - - - - - - - - - - - - - - .]Ι̣Α̣[- - - - - - - - - - - - - - - - - -] [*in rasura*]
[- - - - - - - - - - - - - - -] ἐ̣π̣ε̣ψ[ήφιζεν - - - - - - - - - - -] [*in rasura*]

Another fragment, **71** (below), found at almost the same time and in approximately the same area, appears to have a different line length and thus to derive from a separate decree of about the same date. However, the coincidence of script, marble, and findspot suggests that these two fragments may derive from the same monument, perhaps from different faces of the stele.

79. Meritt (1981, pp. 85, 88–89, 95) places him in 253/2; Osborne (1989, pp. 221–225; also 2000, p. 508) argues for 243/2 (see also *SEG* XXXIX 131, XLIX 8, and L 1). Tracy (*AAM*, pp. 114 and 168) is undecided.

80. The Athenian form of this name, Dieitrephes, is attested in several Attic demes: see *LGPN* II, p. 115.

Figure 71. Fragment from the conclusion of a decree (71)

71 Fragment from the conclusion of a decree — Fig. 71

I 2747b. A fragment of a stele of micaceous Pentelic marble discovered on April 13, 1935, near the Odeion giants (M 9) in rubble from previous excavations. It is broken all around and on the back, where some mortar adheres.

H. 0.11, W. 0.12, Th. 0.02; L.H. 0.007–0.008; non-stoich. vert. 0.015.

Before the mid-3rd century B.C. — Non-stoich. ca. 42–45

[- -]
[τὸν γραμματέα τὸν κατὰ πρυ]ṭ<α>νẹ[ίαν καὶ στῆσαι ἐν ἀ]-
[κροπόλει· εἰς δὲ τὴν ἀναγράφ]ḥν τῆ[ς στήλης - - - - - - - - -]
[- - - - - - - - - - - - - - - - - - - -] δράχ̣μα[ς ἐκ τῶν εἰς τὰ κατὰ]
[ψηφίσματα ἀναλισκομένων τῶι] δ̣ήμωι [*vacat*]
vacat

This is by the same hand as **70** (above), but appears to have a different line length.

Line 1: At the left, the base of the vertical of tau survives, followed by the two diagonals of an alpha, but with no trace of the crossbar. Nu is complete and is followed by the lower part of the vertical of epsilon.

Line 2: The right hasta of eta partially survives in the first stoichos, its top and bottom hidden by the abrasion, and with no trace of the horizontal.

Line 3: The outline of a delta is visible, framed by the mortar that adheres to the stone.

Line 4: The middle of the right diagonal of delta survives.

72 Fragment of an honorific decree — Fig. 72

I 1363. A fragment of a stele of micaceous Pentelic marble discovered on February 23, 1934, in a well on the east slope of Kolonos Agoraios, below the Hephaisteion (G 8:1), in a Byzantine context. It is broken all around and on the back.

H. 0.104, W. 0.07, Th. 0.072; L.H. 0.006; non-stoich. vert. 0.0098.

Before the mid-3rd century B.C.? Non-stoich.

[- -]
[- - - . . ⁵ . .]ΣΚΙ[- - - - - - - - - - - - - - - - - - - -]
[- - - . . . .]Ι[[ΧΡΩ]]Ο[- - - - - - - - - - - - - - - - -]
[- - - . . . .]ΟΝΕΠ[- - - - - - - - - - - - - - - - - - -]
[- - - εἰς τ]ὴν φ[[υ]]λα[κὴν? - - - - - - - - - - - - -]
[- - - . . .]ΩΝΑΣΤΡΑ[- - - - - - - - - - - - - - - - -]
[- - - . . ἐ]κ τῶν ἰδ[ίων - - - - - - - - - - - - - - - -]
[- - - . . ⁵ . .]ΧΡΥ[- - - - - - - - - - - - - - - - - - -]
[- -]

Figure 72. Fragment of an honorific decree (72)

Lines 1–4 and lines 5–7 may be the work of two different masons: the rho of line 2 has a much larger loop than that of the rhos of lines 5 and 7. The spacing between lines 4 and 5 is 0.005, greater than that between other lines, suggesting that a new document began in line 5.

Line 1: The end of a very flat diagonal, the lower half of kappa, and the base of a vertical are preserved.

Line 2: A vertical stroke is partly visible to left of the chi; chi, rho, and omega are clumsy corrections of something previously inscribed here, perhaps gamma, chi, and eta. To right of omega, the left side of a circular letter is partly visible.

Line 3: The first vertical and part of the horizontal of pi survive.

Line 4: In the fourth stoichos the mason first inscribed a lambda, then corrected it to an upsilon.

Line 5: The bottom of the right loop of omega survives.

Line 6: The tip of the upper diagonal of kappa is preserved.

Line 7: The upper two-thirds of each of these letters survives.

The character of the script suggests that the date is the first half of the 3rd century B.C., when such "disjointed" lettering is most common.

Line 4: For this phrase, cf. *IG* II² 283, line 12.

73 Fragment of a decree Fig. 73

I 2721. A fragment of a stele of Pentelic marble discovered on April 2, 1935, over the east part of the Middle Stoa (N 12), in a modern wall. It is broken all around. The back is rough-picked, but probably as a result of reworking and not original.

H. 0.135, W. 0.072, Th. 0.062; L.H. 0.006–0.007; non-stoich. vert. ca. 0.012; the horizontal spacing is irregular.

Before the mid-3rd century B.C.? Non-stoich. ca. 38–40

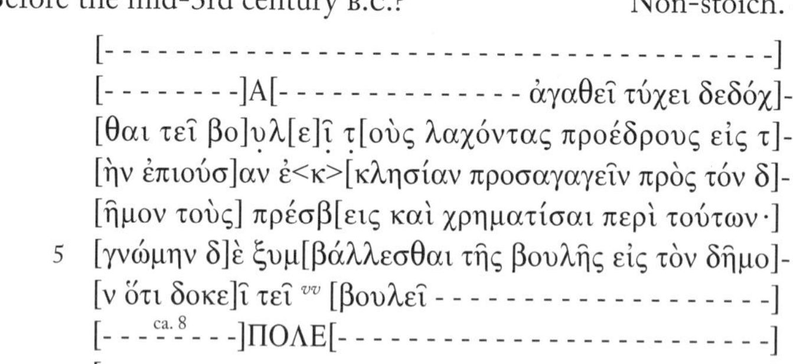

[- -]
[- - - - - - - -]Α[- - - - - - - - - - - - - - ἀγαθεῖ τύχει δεδόχ]-
[θαι τεῖ βο]υλ[ε]ῖ τ[οὺς λαχόντας προέδρους εἰς τ]-
[ὴν ἐπιούσ]αν ἐ<κ>[κλησίαν προσαγαγεῖν πρὸς τόν δ]-
[ῆμον τοὺς] πρέσβ[εις καὶ χρηματίσαι περὶ τούτων·]
[γνώμην δ]ὲ ξυμ[βάλλεσθαι τῆς βουλῆς εἰς τὸν δῆμο]-
[ν ὅτι δοκε]ῖ τεῖ vv [βουλεῖ - - - - - - - - - - - - - - - - - -]
[- - - ca. 8 - - -]ΠΟΛΕ[- -]
[- -]

Figure 73. Fragment of a decree (73)

Line 2: The vertical of upsilon survives; after the lambda, epsilon is not preserved, but the bases of iota and of the vertical of tau are visible.

Line 3: The diagonals of kappa were never inscribed.

Line 6: After the second iota there appear to be two uninscribed spaces, where one might expect the first two letters of the word βουλεῖ.

The hand is characteristic of the first half of the 3rd century B.C.

74 Fragment of a decree — Fig. 74

I 5317. A fragment of a stele of micaceous Pentelic marble discovered on March 17, 1938, west of the Panathenaic Way and northwest of the Eleusinion (S 18), in a Byzantine context. It is broken all around and on the back.

H. 0.088, W. 0.088, Th. 0.048; L.H. 0.005; stoich. 0.013 (square).

Before the mid-3rd century B.C.? — Stoich.

[- -]
[Ἐλαφηβ]ολ̣ι̣[ῶνος - - - - - - - - - τῆς πρυτανείας - - - - - - -]
[. . ⁵ . . τ]ῶμ πρ[οέδρων ἐπεψήφιζεν - - - - - - - - - - - - - - - -]
[. . ⁵ . . ι]ος *vv* ἔ[δοξεν τεῖ βουλεῖ καὶ τῶι δήμωι - - - - - - -]
[. Περγα]σεὺ̣ς ε[ἶπεν· -]
[. . . ⁶ . . .] ο̣ ι̣ερε̣[ὺς -]
[- -]

Line 1: The bases of the diagonals of lambda and of a central vertical are visible after omicron.

Line 3: The right side of the face is abraded, but the epsilon, though faint, is clear.

Line 4: After the first epsilon the left diagonal of what appears to be an upsilon survives; after this the tips of the outer diagonals of sigma are visible.

Line 5: The upper right curve of omicron, the top of iota, and the upper left corner of the second epsilon are preserved.

I believe, on the basis of the shapes of epsilon, mu, sigma, and omega, that this may be the work of the "Cutter of Agora I 3238 and I 4169," active between 286/5 and 245/4 B.C.[81] The stoichedon layout of the text suggests that it was engraved fairly early in this mason's career.

Line 3: For the omission of the phrase καὶ συμπρόεδροι, cf. *Agora* XVI, no. 172, line 4.

Figure 74. Fragment of a decree (74)

81. See n. 78, above.

75 Fragment of an honorific decree Fig. 75

I 5391. A fragment of a stele of Pentelic marble discovered on April 15, 1938, over a revetted basin south of the Eleusinion (T 21), in a Late Roman context. It is broken all around and on the back. Tracy published this in 2003.[82]

H. 0.069, W. 0.039, Th. 0.011; L.H. 0.007; stoich. 0.014 (square).

Before the mid-3rd century B.C.? Stoich.

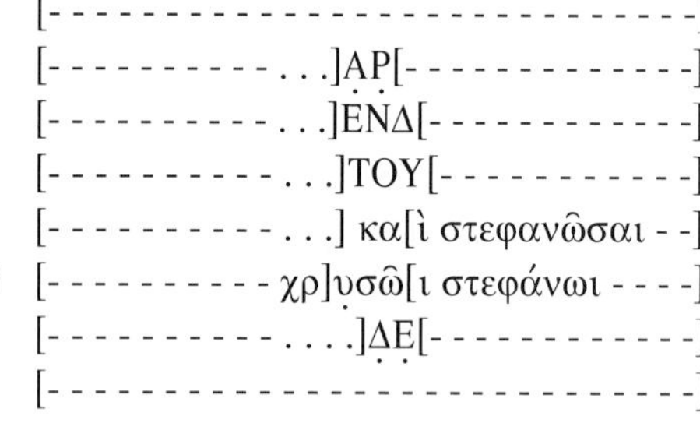
[- -]
[- - - - - - - - - - . . .]Α̣Ρ̣[- - - - - - - - - - - - -]
[- - - - - - - - - - . . .]ΕΝΔ[- - - - - - - - - - - -]
[- - - - - - - - - - - . . .]ΤΟΥ[- - - - - - - - - - -]
[- - - - - - - - - - - . . .] κα[ὶ στεφανῶσαι - -]
[- - - - - - - - - χρ]υ̣σῶ[ι στεφάνωι - - - -]
[- - - - - - - - - - - - . . . .]Δ̣Ε̣[- - - - - - - - - - - -]
[- -]

Figure 75. Fragment of an honorific decree (75)

Line 1: The bases of the diagonals of alpha and of the vertical of rho survive in the break. Tracy does not print this line.

Line 2: The bottom left corner of delta is visible. Tracy prints this as a dotted alpha.

Lines 4 and 5: In each of these lines the left side of the next stoichos survives uninscribed to right of the last inscribed letter, suggesting that the next letter, in each case, was iota.

Line 5: The tip of the right diagonal of upsilon survives. Tracy prints only sigma and omega.

Line 6: The apex of delta and the upper left corner of epsilon are preserved. Tracy does not print this line.

The letter shapes are distinctive and some, in particular epsilon, kappa, and omega, are much like those of the "Cutter of Agora I 3238 and I 4169";[83] however, alpha, nu, omicron, sigma, and upsilon are less like this mason's work. Tracy may be correct, however, in attributing this fragment to the "Cutter of *IG* II[2] 657," active between ca. 305 and ca. 275 B.C.[84]

76 Fragment of a decree Fig. 76

I 5747. A fragment of a stele of micaceous Pentelic marble discovered on March 30, 1939, in a well west of the Panathenaic Way and southwest of the Eleusinion (S 22:2), in a context of the 7th century A.D. The smooth-dressed left side is preserved, with a left margin of 0.014.

H. 0.088, W. 0.088, Th. 0.054; L.H. 0.006; semi-stoich. vert. 0.017; the horizontal spacing between letters is ca. 0.005.

Before the mid-3rd century B.C.? Semi-stoich.

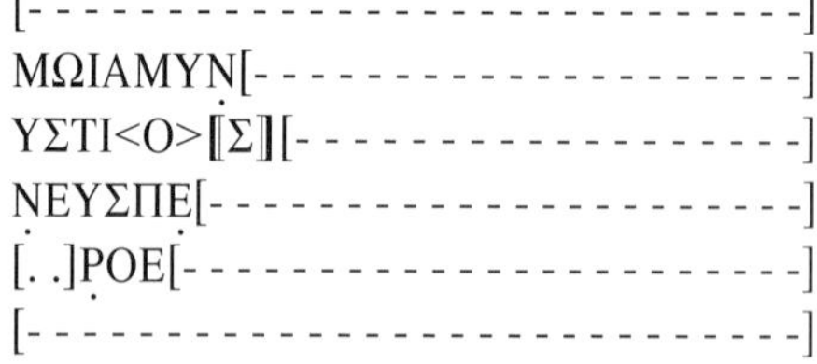
[- -]
ΜΩΙΑΜΥΝ̣[- - - - - - - - - - - - - - - - - - -]
ΥΣΤΙ<Ο>⟦Σ⟧[- - - - - - - - - - - - - - - - -]
Ν̣ΕΥΣΠΕ̣[- - - - - - - - - - - - - - - - - - - -]
[. .]Ρ̣ΟΕ[- -]
[- -]

Line 1: In the seventh stoichos the base of the first vertical of a nu is preserved.

82. *AAM,* pp. 68–69, no. 2; photograph, p. 70, fig. 15.

83. See n. 78, above.

84. *AAM,* pp. 62–73; photograph of *IG* II[2] 657 (squeeze), p. 63, fig. 11.

Figure 76. Fragment of a decree (76)

Line 2: The mason inscribed a theta instead of an omicron, and followed this with a sigma that is quite unlike the first sigma in this line and the one in line 3. I believe that he wrote theta-epsilon first, then corrected the epsilon to a sigma, but did not bother to erase the dot of the theta.

Line 3: The top of the right vertical of nu survives.

Line 4: The top of the loop of rho and the upper half of omicron survive.

The lettering is distinctive, but I have been unable to find its match in other documents; however, it seems most characteristic of the first half of the 3rd century B.C.

Line 1: [ἔδοξεν τεῖ βουλεῖ καὶ τῶι δή]|μωι· Ἀμυν̣[- - εἶπεν]?[85]

Line 2: The name [Καρ]|ύστι<ο>⟦ς⟧?[86] Alternatively, the demotic [Ἀναφλ]|ύστι<ο>⟦ς⟧?

Line 4: [τοὺ|ς π]ρ̣οέ[δρους], or [π]ρ̣οε[δρεύειν]?

77 Fragment from the conclusion of a decree Fig. 77

I 5364. A fragment of a stele of white-flecked gray Hymettian marble discovered on April 2, 1938, southeast of the Market Square, over the Panathenaic Way (R 17), in a modern wall. The pick-dressed right side and convex, rough-picked back are preserved. The right margin is 0.028, and there is a vertical, uninscribed space of 0.025 below the last line.

H. 0.13, W. 0.09, Th. 0.079; L.H. 0.004–0.006; non-stoich. vert. 0.012.

Ca. 262–250 B.C.? Non-stoich. ca. 29

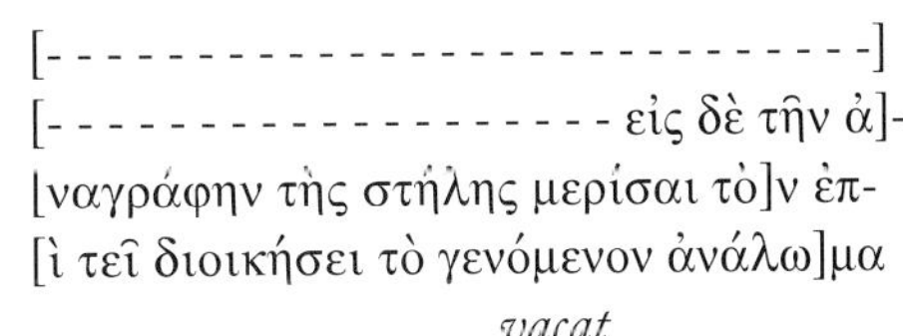

[- -]
[- - - - - - - - - - - - - - - - - - - εἰς δὲ τὴν ἀ]-
[ναγράφην τῆς στήλης μερίσαι τὸ]ν ἐπ-
[ὶ τεῖ διοικήσει τὸ γενόμενον ἀνάλω]μα
vacat

The right margin is unusually wide, if this is part of a decree.

The hand seems appropriate to the second quarter of the 3rd century B.C.

Lines 1–2: By this restoration the presence of the Single Officer of Administration as the person responsible for meeting the cost of engravure,

85. Amyntas is attested in Anaphlystos, so far only in the Roman era, but this is only one of several possibilities; perhaps a longer name should be sought, such as Amynandros, or Amynomenos, or Amyntichos, all of which are attested for the 4th century B.C. and perhaps later; see *LGPN* II, p. 26.

86. Attested for Athens in the 6th century B.C.; see *LGPN* II, p. 256.

Figure 77. Fragment from the conclusion of a decree (77)

in combination with the phrase τὸ γενόμενον ἀνάλωμα, places this decree in the period after 262/1 B.C. and the end of the Chremonidean War.[87]

78 Fragment of a decree Fig. 78

I 5813. A fragment of a stele of pale gray Hymettian marble discovered on May 11, 1939, west of the Eleusinion and the Panathenaic Way (R 20), in a late context. It is broken all around and on the back.

H. 0.088, W. 0.12, Th. 0.052; L.H. 0.005; non-stoich. vert. 0.013.

Ca. 255–235 B.C.? Non-stoich.

[- -]

[- - - - . . .]ΟΠΛΙΤ̣[- - - - - - - - - - - - - -]

[- - - -]Ο̣ΛΑΒΕΙΝΙΤΟ[- - - - - - - - - - - -]

[- - - -]ΘΑΙΛ̣Ε̣ΛΕΙΤ[- - - - - - - - - - - - -]

[- - - - . .]Ο̣ΤΑΣΠΙ̣Σ[- - - - - - - - - - - - -]

[- -]

The crossbar of each alpha is extremely faint.

Line 1: The base of the vertical of tau survives.

Line 2: The lower curve of omicron is preserved before the lambda.

Line 3: The fourth letter may be a lambda, or a delta whose base has been omitted; after it, the vertical of what is likely an epsilon survives, but the rest of this letter is hidden by an abrasion.

Line 4: The top half of a circular letter is preserved in the first stoichos; the top of iota and the upper diagonals of sigma survive after the pi.

Alpha is relatively wide, its left diagonal slightly shorter and its horizontal faint and sloping slightly up to right; the ends of the horizontals of epsilon thicken, and the middle one is quite short; omicron is medium-sized and not quite round; the horizontal of pi overlaps its first vertical; and sigma has almost flat outer diagonals and inner diagonals not meeting exactly but overlapping. These characteristics are

87. See Henry 1984, pp. 74–81.

Figure 78. Fragment of a decree (78)

found also in the hand of the "Cutter of *IG* II² 788," who was active between ca. 255/4 and 235/4 B.C.,[88] and I believe, therefore, that this fragment may be his work.

Line 2: [ἀπ]ọλάβειν or [ὑπ]ọλάβειν?

79 Fragment of a decree Fig. 79

I 1983. A fragment of a stele of Hymettian marble discovered on May 14, 1934, in the area of the Tholos, in a marble dump. It is broken all around and on the back.

H. 0.099, W. 0.115, Th. 0.01; L.H. 0.004; non-stoich. vert. 0.009; the horizontal spacing is ca. 0.003–0.004.

Ca. 255–235 B.C.? Non-stoich.

[- -]
[- - - - - . . . ⁷ . . .]ḲOỴ[- - - - - - - - - - - - - - - - -]
[- - - - - . . ⁵ . .] τὸ ψήφι[σμα - - - - - - - - - - - - -]
[- - - - - ἐψη]φίσθα[ι] τῆị [βουλῆι? - - - - - - - -]
[- -]

Figure 79. Fragment of a decree (79)

88. Tracy 1988, pp. 311–322; description of the letter forms, pp. 311–312; photograph, pl. 86; see now *AAM*, pp. 128–149.

Figure 80. Fragment of a decree (reaffirming a grant of citizenship?) (80)

Line 1: The lower diagonal of a kappa or chi survives; the angle is too flat for this to be part of an alpha or lambda. The circular second letter has no dot; after it, the bottom of a vertical is visible, too far to the right to be that of an iota, with traces on the break that suggest the junction of the diagonals of an upsilon.

Line 3: At the right edge the stone breaks on the vertical of iota.

The mason who engraved this fragment was evidently at pains to make his text look regular, almost stoichedon. This is typical of the "Cutter of *IG* II² 788." Also characteristic of this mason are those letters that survive here, notably theta, sigma, and phi.[89]

80 Fragment of a decree (reaffirming a grant of citizenship?) Fig. 80

I 5752. A fragment of a stele of blue-gray, white-flecked Hymettian marble discovered on March 29, 1939, at the north foot of the Areopagus (G 19), in the foundation wall of the Church of Ayios Athanasios. The pick-dressed left side is preserved, with a margin of ca. 0.003.

H. 0.091, W. 0.22, Th. 0.095; L.H. 0.004–0.005; non-stoich. vert. 0.0105.

Ca. 255–235 B.C.? Non-stoich. ca. 48–50

[- -]
[.]Τ̣ΕΙ̣Α[- -]
[.]Ο̣ΥΣΚΑ[. . .]ΕΕ[- ὅπως ἐφά]-
μ̣ιλλον εἶ πᾶσιν [τοῖς φ]ι̣λο[τιμουμένοις - - - - - - - - - - - - - - - - - - -]
Ρ̣ΕΙΝ· ἀγαθεῖ τύχει· δεδόχθα̣[ι τεῖ βουλεῖ τοὺς λάχοντας προέδρους]
[εἰ]ς̣ τὴ[ν ἐ]πίουσαν ἐκκλησία[ν χρηματίσαι περὶ - - - - - - - - γνώμην]
δ̣ὲ̣ ξ[υμβάλλ]εσθαι τῆς [βου]λ̣ῆς [εἰς τὸν δῆμον ὅτι δοκεῖ τεῖ βουλεῖ]
[- - - ca. 10–11 - - -]Υ̣Α̣Θ̣Η̣Ν̣[- -]
[- -]

Line 1: The lower halves of these four letters survive.

Line 3: The base of the fourth diagonal of mu is preserved.

Line 4: The upper right side of the loop of rho survives; at the right edge the base of the left diagonal of alpha is visible.

Line 5: The upper two diagonals of sigma survive in the first preserved stoichos.

89. See n. 88, above.

Line 6: The apex of delta, the upper left corner of epsilon, and the xi are preserved; the apex of the lambda is visible. At the right edge the apex of lambda survives before eta and sigma.

Line 7: There are faint traces of the tops of letters where the stone has broken away: the tips of the upper diagonals of upsilon or chi; the apex of a triangular letter; the upper curve of a round letter; and the tops of three verticals, perhaps iota and eta, or eta and iota or nu.

The hand seems much like that of the "Cutter of *IG* II² 788."[90] Note, in particular, the shapes of alpha, epsilon, kappa, and sigma.

Line 1: [πολι]τẹίạ[ν]? Perhaps a reference to an earlier award of citizenship?

Lines 2–3: Cf. *IG* II² 1227, lines 20–21.

81 Fragment of a decree (of a deme?) Fig. 81

I 935. The upper left corner of a stele of blue, white-flecked Hymettian marble discovered on June 5, 1933, east of the Tholos (H 11), in a marble dump from the late wall. The rough-picked back and stipple-dressed left side are preserved, as well as a crowning molding, double-tiered horizontal taenia, and part of the gable and central akroterion of the pedimental top. The left margin is 0.014.

Figure 81. Fragment of a decree (of a deme?) (81)

90. See n. 88, above.

The surviving left half of the stele is 0.26 wide from the edge to the center of the gable, so that its full width would have been ca. 0.52, allowing for a line of about 33–34 letters if the right margin was the same width as the left.

H. 0.398 (molding 0.012, taenia 0.06, pediment 0.148), W. 0.27, Th. 0.139 (projection of taenia 0.023); L.H. 0.006–0.007; stoich. hor. 0.0145, vert. 0.0155. There is a vertical uninscribed space of 0.015 above line 1.

Ca. 255–235 B.C. Stoich.

[Ἀγ]αθεῖ Τ[ύχει?]
[.]ΗΔΙΩΝ[- - - - - - - - - - - - - - - - - - -]
ΤΑΙΣΕ̣[- -]
ΕΠΕΙ̣[- -]
ΓΕΝ[- -]
ΕΥΕΠ̣[- -]
ΠΟΤ[- -]
ΤΗ[- -]
ΞΥ̣[- -]
[- -]

Line 3: The upper left corner of an epsilon (or a gamma, or pi?) survives.

Line 4: The top of the iota survives.

Line 6: At the right a left vertical is preserved in the break, perhaps that of a pi.

Line 9: The xi appears to be set off a little to the left; the tip of the left diagonal of upsilon survives.

The hand seems appropriate to the third quarter of the 3rd century B.C. Note the very broad lettering; the tendency for straight strokes to be slightly curved; the faintness and slight slant up to right of the horizontal of alpha; the thickening of the ends of the horizontals of epsilon, the inner considerably shorter; the slope of the horizontal of pi, overlapping the second vertical; the almost flat outer diagonals of sigma, their ends thickened but not serifed; the way in which the vertical of upsilon projects below the baseline; and the omega, which is almost a full circle with upward-pointing extenders. These characteristics, I believe, are found in the non-stoichedon *IG* II^2 798 (EM 7449 + 7455), attributed by Tracy to the "Cutter of *IG* II^2 788."[91]

Line 2: [Μ]ηδίων (or [Μ]η<λ>ίων?) [εἶπεν]?

Line 3: [ἔδοξεν (or δεδόχθαι) τοῖς δημο]ταῖς· ἐ̣[παινέσαι - -]?

Line 4: ἐπει̣[δή]?

Line 5: γεν[όμενος]? Cf. *IG* II^2 1261, lines 4 and 46.

Line 6: εὖ ἐπ̣[εμελήθη τῆς θυσίας τῆς - - -]? Cf. *IG* II^2 1261, lines 46–47.

Line 7: [ὑ]|πὸ τ[- -]?

82 Fragment from the conclusion of a decree conferring citizenship — Fig. 82

I 6759. A fragment of a stele of pale gray, white-flecked Hymettian marble discovered in the winter of 1956/1957, in the garden area south of the Temple of Hephaistos (D–E 10–11). It is broken all around and on the back.

91. See n. 88, above.

The upper left part of an engraved myrtle wreath survives at bottom left.

H. 0.079, W. 0.059, Th. 0.027; L.H. 0.0045; non-stoich. vert. 0.011.

End of 3rd century B.C. Non-stoich. ca. 54–57

καὶ στ[ῆσαι]
13 π̣ρὸς τῶι Ἐλευσινίωι· [εἰς δ]<u>ε̣ τ̣ὴ̣ν ἀν</u>[αγράφην καὶ τὴν ἀνάθεσιν τῆς στήλης]
14 [μ]ε̣ρίσαι τὸ γενόμενον [ἀν]<u>α̣λωμα το̣</u>[ν ταμίαν τῶν στρατιωτικῶν *vacat*]
wreath [*wreath*?]

The text of the new fragment is underlined.

Line 13 (= line 1 of I 6759): The lowest horizontal of epsilon and the bases of the verticals of tau and eta are visible in the abraded area at left.

Line 14: The base of the right diagonal of the first alpha survives at left. At the right edge the stone breaks on the upper left curve of a circular letter.

Figure 82. Fragment from the conclusion of a decree conferring citizenship (82)

This is part of *Agora* XVI, no. 239 (I 4260 + 5327), which is dated to the end of the 3rd century B.C. and is an award of myrtle crowns and grants of citizenship to several persons.[92] It does not join the lower right side of I 4260, lines 13–14, but is separated from it by a space of ca. 3–4 letters. The text of this decree was inscribed upon a stele whose foliation is almost vertical to the face, so that it has broken into fragments having almost perpendicular sides. A narrow splinter has evidently broken away from the right side of I 4260 or the left side of I 6759 and is now lost. The three fragments of this document were found at different times and quite widely separated from one another, fragment *a* in grid square N 15, fragment *b* in grid square T 21, and the new fragment in grid square D–E 10–11.

83 Fragment of a decree Fig. 83

I 6409. A fragment of a stele of Pentelic marble discovered on July 10, 1951, in the Roman building northeast of the Civic Offices (J 12). The smooth-dressed left side is preserved, with a margin of 0.014. The right edge has been reworked and is also smooth-dressed.

H. 0.078, W. 0.095, Th. 0.085; L.H. 0.006–0.007; stoich. hor. 0.0125, vert. 0.0135.

3rd–2nd century B.C.? Stoich.

[- -]
ONỊ[- -]
ΠΑΔΑΡ[- -]
ΙΑΝΤΟ[- -]
ΙΩΝΗΣỊ[- -]
[- -]

Line 1: The base of a vertical survives at the right edge, too close to the nu to be part of an upsilon.

Line 2: The vertical and the lower part of the loop of rho are preserved.

Line 4: The top of a vertical is visible at the right edge after sigma.

The letter forms are highly distinctive: note how one end of a straight stroke is very shallow, the other much deeper, with a tendency to thicken into a blob; the way in which the diagonals of alpha and delta form a cross at the apex; how the horizontal bar of alpha and eta is slightly slanted and overlaps the right edge

92. Photographs of Agora I 4260 and I 5327: *Agora* XVI, pl. 25; on the significance of crowns of myrtle, see Walbank 2002, p. 65, no. 8.

Figure 83. Fragment of a decree (83)

of the letter; the extension of the horizontal of pi beyond the second vertical; and the omega, which is inscribed as a circle to which horizontal extenders are added, the right one higher than the left. Collectively, these traits seem characteristic of the late 3rd or early 2nd century B.C.

Line 2: [λαμ]|παδαρ[χοῦντος]?

84 Fragment of a decree granting *enktesis* Fig. 84

I 5767. A fragment of a stele of micaceous Pentelic marble discovered on April 3, 1939, at the north foot of the Areopagus (Q_23), in a Late Roman context. The tooth-dressed left side is preserved, with a left margin of 0.01.

H. 0.086, W. 0.09, Th. 0.073; L.H. 0.006; stoich. hor. 0.011, vert. 0.012.

3rd–2nd century B.C.? Stoich.

[- -]
ε̣ῖ[ν]α̣ι̣ δὲ [- -]
I δὲ ἔ[[γ]]κ[τησιν -]
TI[[M]]HΣΟ̣[- -]
THNT[- -]
EΦΑ̣[- -]
[- -]

Figure 84. Fragment of a decree granting *enktesis* (84)

Line 1: The lower left corner of epsilon and the base of a central vertical survive in the first two stoichoi; in the fourth and fifth stoichoi the bases of the diagonals of alpha or lambda and of a central vertical are preserved; after the delta the lower left corner of epsilon survives in the break.

Line 2: Gamma is the correction of a mistake, perhaps of two mistakes, since in this stoichos there seem to be a very narrow nu and also an omicron, in addition to gamma.

Line 3: Mu is larger and more deeply cut than other letters in this line and is the correction of a mistake; after eta, the photograph shows a long, slightly slanting stroke, but this is a random mark, cutting through the end of the top diagonal of sigma; sigma itself is damaged, but almost complete. After this, the upper curve of a circular letter survives.

Line 5: The apex of a triangular letter is preserved after phi.

The hand is a distinctive one, but hard to match: it seems appropriate to the second half of the 3rd century B.C. or a little later.

Lines 2–3: [γῆς μὲν μέχρι - -]| τι[[μ]]ῆς, ο̣[ἰκίας δὲ - -]? Cf. *IG* II² 810, line 2. Grants of *enktesis* with the value expressly stated in various ways occur through the second half of the 3rd and into the 2nd century B.C.[93]

Figure 85. Fragment of a decree (85)

85 Fragment of a decree Fig. 85

I 1083. A fragment of a stele of light gray Hymettian marble discovered on October 19, 1933, in the northwest corner of the Market Square (G–K 5–8), in a marble dump. The rough-picked back may be original. Parts of the crowning molding, horizontal taenia, and tympanon of the pediment are preserved.

H. 0.178 (molding lower register 0.034, molding upper register 0.034, taenia 0.012, pediment 0.028), W. 0.106, Th. 0.160 (projection of taenia 0.028); L.H. 0.007; non-stoich., horizontal spacing 0.003.

3rd–2nd century B.C.? Non-stoich.

[ἐπὶ] Διονυ[σίου ἄρχοντος? - - - - - - - - - - - - - -]
[- -]

Line 1: In the photograph there appears to be a very clear iota before the delta, but this is actually a deep fracture in the stone, not part of any letter.

From the very small sample of letters available, the hand seems appropriate to the late 3rd or early 2nd century B.C.[94]

If this is correctly restored as part of an archon formula, Dionysios could be the archon of either 202/1 or even 194/3 B.C.[95]

Figure 86. Fragment of a decree (concerning an embassy?) (86)

86 Fragment of a decree (concerning an embassy?) Fig. 86

I 1449. A fragment of a stele of blue-gray Hymettian marble discovered on March 3, 1934, north of the Tholos (G 11), in a late context. The stipple-dressed left side is preserved, with a drafted edge 0.01 wide adjoining the face. The left margin is 0.007.

H. 0.064, W. 0.037, Th. 0.067; L.H. 0.006; non-stoich. vert. 0.013.

3rd–2nd century B.C.? Non-stoich.

[- -]
Ι̣Λ̣[- -]
τῶ̣ι [- πρεσ]-
βεὺς [- -]
ΠΕΙΘ̣[- -]
Α̣Γ̣[- -]
[- -]

Line 1: The bases of a vertical and the diagonals of alpha or lambda survive.

Line 4: The left side of a circular letter is preserved.

Line 5: The open apex of a triangular letter survives, followed by the upper left corner of a gamma, epsilon, or pi.

93. See Pečírka 1966, pp. 156–157.

94. See *ALC*, passim.

95. For the dates, see Meritt 1977, pp. 179–181.

Figure 87. Fragment of a decree (87)

The lettering closely resembles that of the "Cutter of Agora I 656 + 6355," active between 203/2 and 164/3 B.C.,[96] but there are too few letters to allow definite attribution to this mason.

Line 5: [ἀπ]|αγ[γέλλει?]?

87 Fragment of a decree

Fig. 87

I 5171. A fragment of a stele of reddish-gray Hymettian marble discovered on January 26, 1938, west of the Eleusinion over the Panathenaic Way (S 19), in an Ottoman context. The top of a pedimental stele survives, preserving the central akroterion and the spring of the crowning molding, although the pediment itself has been destroyed. The rough-picked back is preserved.

H. 0.277 (molding and pediment 0.09), W. 0.13, Th. 0.145 (projection of molding 0.015); L.H. 0.005–0.006; non-stoich. vert. 0.092.

The width of the stele can be estimated from the height of the pediment as ca. 0.65, allowing for a line of up to ca. 60 letters.

96. *ALC,* pp. 82–88; description of lettering, pp. 82–83; photograph, p. 83, fig. 8.

3rd–2nd century B.C.? Non-stoich. ca. 56–60?

[ἐπὶ ----------- ἄρχοντος, ἐπὶ] τ̣ῆς Οἰνεΐδ[ος ------------- -πρυτανείας, ἧι]
[----------------- ἐγ Μυρρ]ινούττης ἐ[γραμμάτευεν, -----------------]
[----------------------- μ]ι̣ᾶι καὶ εἰκό[στει τῆς πρυτανείας· ἐκκλ]-
[ησία κυρία ἐν τῶι θεάτρωι· τῶν π]ροέδρων ἐπε̣[ψήφιζεν -------------------]
[----------------- καὶ συμπ]ρόεδροι vv ἔδ[οξεν τεῖ βουλεῖ καὶ τῶι δήμωι ---]
[------------------------]Λ̣ΙΕΥΣ εἶπε[ν -------------------------]
[------------------------]βουλ⟦εῖ⟧ vvv τοὺ[ς <προέδρους τοὺς> λάχοντας προεδρεύ]-
[ειν εἰς τὴν ἐπιοῦσαν ἐκκλησίαν] προσαγάγειν Π[------------------------]
[-----------------------] ο̣ἱ̣ θεοὶ προσέτα[ξαν --------------------]
[-----------------------] Λ̣Υ̣ΡΙΚΑ[. .]ΕΙΚΟ[---------------------]
[----------------------- τ]ῆι σωτηρίαι τῆς π̣[όλεως? ---------------]
[---------------------- Ἀ]λ̣α̣ιεὺς εἶπεν̣· κ̣ατ[----------------------]
[------------------------]ι̣ καὶ τ'ἄλλα καὶ ΣΚ̣Ε̣[------------------]
[------------------------]Ι̣ΛΗΦΕΙ[. . . .]ΚΙΣΑΝ[-------------------]
[-----------------------] δ̣οκεῖ τεῖ βουλεῖ v ΕΠ[-------------------]
[-----------------------] σ̣ω̣τ̣[ῆρ]ο̣ς̣ Ε̣[Ι]ΣΕ[---------------------]
[---------------------------------]ΙΑΣ[-----------------------]
[---]

Line 1: The right tip of the horizontal of tau survives; the sigma lies just to the right of the center of the stele.

Line 4: The vertical of the third epsilon is preserved at the right, with abrasions to the right of it.

Line 6: In the first stoichos the lower part of a right diagonal survives, with no trace of a base; thus it could be either alpha or lambda, but not delta.

Line 7: Epsilon and iota are inscribed *in rasura.*

Line 9: In the first two preserved stoichoi the upper right curve of a circular letter and a vertical survive, both indistinct.

Line 11: The lower parts of the verticals of pi survive.

Line 12: In the first two preserved stoichoi the apex of a triangular letter and the diagonals of another are visible.

Line 13: The bottom of a vertical is visible in the first stoichos; in the last an abrasion obscures parts of two letters, the first of which may be a kappa or an epsilon, while the second may be an epsilon; the verticals of these letters can be discerned with difficulty.

Line 14: The bottom of a vertical survives, followed by the faint outline of a lambda.

Line 15: The lower right corner of delta survives; the remaining letters in this line are very faint, but their outlines survive.

Line 16: The upper diagonals of sigma, the upper curve of omega, and the top half of tau are preserved; the next two letters have been destroyed; after them the upper curve of an omicron and the upper three diagonals of sigma survive; after the sigma a horizontal mark may be the upper horizontal of an epsilon; the stoichos following this is obscured by mortar, but the spacing suggests that an iota may have been carved here. After this, sigma and epsilon are clearly visible.

Line 17: These letters are very faint; they lie below the omicron, sigma, and epsilon of line 16.

The script suggests a date from the end of the 3rd to the early part of the 2nd century B.C. It appears close to the work of the "Cutter of Agora I 7181," active between 224/3 and 188/7 B.C.;[97] note the shapes of alpha, gamma, epsilon, nu, sigma, tau, and upsilon; the tendency to attach small serifs to terminal

97. *ALC,* pp. 61–67; description of lettering, pp. 61–62; photograph, p. 62, fig. 4.

letter strokes; and the relatively wide horizontal spacing. It seems less close to the work of the "Cutter of Agora I 787," active between 229/8 and 218/7 B.C.[98] The deme of the secretary (line 2) is Myrrhinous, belonging to the Phyle Aigeis (II). In the period under consideration, the secretary cycle requires that the secretary be assigned to one of the two years in which the phyle of the secretary is Aigeis (II), but his name and demotic are so far unknown, either 224/3 B.C., the year of the archon Antiphilos, or 211/10 B.C., the year of Aischron.[99] On the evidence of the script, either year is possible.

Line 8: The mason must have omitted the words προέδρους τοὺς (or προεδρεύειν) from line 7; otherwise this line would be far too long.

88 Fragment of a decree — Fig. 88

I 4855. A fragment of a stele of micaceous Pentelic marble discovered on May 11, 1937, south of the Eleusinion (T 21–22), in a late context. It is broken all around and on the back.

H. 0.066, W. 0.068, Th. 0.023; L.H. 0.008; non-stoich. vert. 0.013, horizontal spacing ca. 0.007.

3rd–2nd century B.C.? — Non-stoich.

[- -]
[- - - - - - -]ΑΡΧΑΣ[- - - - - - - - - - - - - - -]
[- - - - - - -]Υ̣ΣΚΑΤ̣[- - - - - - - - - - - - - - -]
[- - - - - - - .]ΕΠΙ[- - - - - - - - - - - - - - - -]
[- - - - - - - .]Ε̣ΘΗ[- - - - - - - - - - - - - - -]
[- -]

Line 1: The left apices of sigma are visible.

Line 2: The right tip of a diagonal survives in the first stoichos; in the fifth stoichos the left tip of the horizontal of tau is visible.

Line 4: Part of an upper horizontal survives, probably of an epsilon.

The alphas with slightly curved horizontals suggest a date in the late 3rd or early 2nd century B.C.

Figure 88. Fragment of a decree (88)

89 Fragment of a decree — Fig. 89

I 3237. A fragment of a stele of Pentelic marble found on September 23, 1935, in the southeast part of the Market Square (N–Q 12–14), in a marble dump. The smooth-dressed left side is preserved.

H. 0.088, W. 0.094, Th. 0.117; L.H. 0.008–0.009; non-stoich. vert. 0.015, horizontal spacing ca. 0.004–0.006.

Beginning of 2nd century B.C. — Non-stoich.

[- -]
Μ̣ΠΟΤ̣[- -]
ΚΗΡΥΚ̣[- -]
ΚΑΙΤ̣[- -]
ΤΗ[- -]
[- -]

Figure 89. Fragment of a decree (89)

98. *ALC*, pp. 41–43; description of lettering on pp. 82–83; photograph on p. 42, fig. 1.

99. See Meritt 1961, pp. 234–235.

Line 1: The base of a slightly sloping right vertical, possibly that of a mu, survives at the right end of the first stoichos; the base of a central vertical is visible in the fourth stoichos.

Line 2: The top of the vertical of the second kappa survives in the break.

Line 3: The left tip of the horizontal of tau survives.

The untidy, disjointed lettering is appropriate to the beginning of the 2nd century B.C., but too few letters survive for attribution to a specific hand.

Lines 1–2: [καὶ τὸν]| κήρυκ̣[α]?

90 Fragment of a decree conferring citizenship Fig. 90

I 6065. A fragment of a stele of very micaceous, pale gray Hymettian marble discovered on August 4, 1947, west of the Civic Offices (I 12), in the Great Drain. The surface is badly abraded. The pick-dressed left side survives, with a left margin of 0.005. The rough-picked back is probably not original.

H. 0.232, W. 0.168, Th. 0.053; L.H. 0.005–0.006; non-stoich. vert. 0.011, horizontal spacing ca. 0.003.

Figure 90. Fragment of a decree conferring citizenship (90)

Ca. 229–190 B.C. Non-stoich. ca. 57–63?

[- -]
[- - - - - - ca. 15–17 - - - - - - -]ΕΛ̣[- -]
[- - - - - - ca. 15–17 - - - - - - -]ΔΩΡ̣[- -]
[- - - - - - ca. 13–15 - - - - -]ΟΥΕΠΙ̣[- -]
ΤΩΙ[- - - ca. 10–12 - - - -] ὅπως δ̣[’ἂν οὖν καὶ ὁ δῆμος ἐμ παντὶ χαιρῶι φαίνηται μεμνή]-
μενος̣ [τῶν] ἐκ[τενῶς τ]ὰς [χρείας αὐτῶι παρεσχημένων, εἶναι αὐτοῖς παρὰ τοῦ δή]-
μ̣ου πολ[ιτε]ί[α]ν καὶ [εἶναι αὐτοῖς δοκιμασθεῖσι γράψασθαι φυλῆς καὶ δήμου καὶ]
φρατρ̣ίας ἧς [ἂ]ν [βού]λ̣ητ̣[αι ἕκαστος· ἀναγράψαι δὲ τόδε τὸ ψήφισμα τὸν γραμμα]-
τέα τὸν̣ κατὰ π[ρυτανείαν εἰς στήλην λιθίνην καὶ στῆσαι ἐν ἀκροπόλει· εἰ]-
ς δὲ τὴν ἀναγ̣[ράφην τῆς στήλης μερίσαι τὸν ταμίαν τῶν στρατιωτικῶν - - ἐ]-
παι̣ν̣έ̣σ̣α̣ι̣ [- -]
ΕΠΙ̣ΜΕ̣Λ[- -]
ΤΑΙ̣ Δ̣Ι̣Ε̣[- -]
ΣΙΑ̣[- -]
[- -]

Line 1: The outlines of an epsilon and of a triangular letter are visible.
Line 2: The base of the vertical of rho survives.
Line 4: The apex of delta is preserved at the right edge.
Line 5: After omicron the curving upper diagonal of sigma is preserved.
Line 6: The fourth diagonal of mu survives.
Line 7: The base of the vertical of the second rho is preserved; at the right edge the bases of lambda and tau survive to either side of the eta.
Line 8: The first three letters are clear; the next eight letters survive, much abraded.
Lines 9–13: The first two letters in each line are clear, but the remainder exist only as faint and abraded outlines.
Tracy attributes this fragment to the "Cutter of *IG* II² 912," who was active between ca. 229/8 and ca. 190 B.C.[100]

Lines 4–7: For these restorations, cf. *Agora* XVI, no. 224, lines 25–27, and *Agora* XVI, no. 239, lines 7–10.

91 Fragment of a decree Fig. 91

I 6306. The upper left corner of a pedimental stele of pale gray, white-flecked Hymettian marble discovered on June 3, 1950, at the west end of the Altar of Ares (L 8), in a Byzantine context. The top and left side are preserved, with a crowning molding and horizontal taenia, the left akroterion, and the central part of the pediment, up to the spring of the central akroterion.

H. 0.192 (molding 0.03, taenia 0.018, pediment 0.078), W. 0.21, Th. 0.074 (projection of taenia 0.02); L.H. 0.007; non-stoich. vert. 0.01.

175/4 or 169/8 B.C. Non-stoich. ca. 40–41?

[Θ] ε [ο ί]
[ἐπὶ . . . .]κ̣ου ἄρχοντ[ος, ἐπὶ τῆς - - - - - - ca. 16 - - - - - -]
[- - - ca. 12 - - - - - -]ε̣ι̣υ̣[- - - - - - - - - ca. 26 - - - - - - - - -]
[- -]

100. *ALC*, pp. 55–60; description of lettering, pp. 55–56; photograph, p. 56, fig. 3.

Figure 91. Fragment of a decree (91)

The line length can be calculated by measuring the distance from the left side to the central akroterion. This allows a width of ca. 0.45 for the pediment, so that the line length will have been ca. 40–41 letters.

Line 1: The epsilon of the invocation survives on the taenia, above the omicron-nu of line 2.

Line 2: The top of a diagonal survives before the first omicron; it may be too steeply angled to be part of a chi or sigma.

Line 3: The upper left corner of epsilon, the top of iota, and the tips of the diagonals of upsilon, survive below the rho, chi, and omicron of line 2, respectively.

The lettering is distinctive, but hard to match; there is a tendency to thicken the free ends of straight strokes; alpha is quite wide, with a slightly sloping and curving bar; all three strokes of nu are the same length, but the diagonal is shallower, and this letter seems to lean backwards; the diameter of omicron is inconsistent, and it is made from several short, straight strokes; the loop of rho is made from several straight strokes, giving it a pennant-like appearance; upsilon is made with a short vertical and long diagonals, extending above the line, and all three strokes are very shallow at one end, deep and thick at the other; the same is true of chi, whose diagonals are each made by two intersecting strokes. I believe that this fragment may be in the style of the "Cutter of Agora I 656 + 6355," but truly diagnostic letters, such as mu and sigma, have not survived.[101]

Line 2: The archon is either Sonikos (of 175/4 B.C.) or Eunikos (of 169/8 B.C.).

101. See n. 96, above.

92 Fragment from the conclusion of a prytany decree, followed by a list of names of councillors — Fig. 92

I 2665. A fragment of a stele of Hymettian marble discovered on March 29, 1935, on the slope of Kolonos Agoraios, ca. 20 southwest of the Tholos (F 12), in a 3rd-century A.D. context. The left side is preserved.

H. 0.153, W. 0.082, Th. 0.065; L.H. 0.005 (lines 1–7), 0.006 (lines 8–9); non-stoich. vert. 0.011.

Ca. 210–170 B.C. — Non-stoich. ca. 65–70

[- -]
Ṇ[- -]
TIΛ̣[- -]
AΦA[- Βε]-
ρενε[ικίδην - καὶ στεφανῶσαι ἕκαστον αὐτῶν θαλ]-
λοῦ σ[τεφάνωι· ἀναγράψαι δὲ τόδε τὸ ψήφισμα τὸν γραμματέα τὸν κατὰ πρυτανείαν εἰς στ]-
⟦ή⟧λην λι[θίνην καὶ στῆσαι ἐν τῶι πρυτανικῶι· τὸ δὲ γενόμενον ἀνάλωμα μερίσαι τὸν ἐπὶ τεῖ]
⟦διοικήσ[ει]⟧]. *vacat*
Διονυσ̣[- -]
Ἁρμο̣δ̣[- -]
[- -]

Line 2: The base of a left diagonal is preserved.

Line 6: In the first stoichos a mu has been partly erased and replaced by an eta.

Line 7: The mason inscribed the phrase τεῖ διοικήσει here, repeating τεῖ from line 6, then erased the whole phrase without completely removing the traces of the original text, and reinscribed διοικήσει *in rasura.*

Line 8: The upper diagonal of sigma survives, though very faint.

Line 9: The upper curve of omicron and the apex of delta are barely visible.

Tracy attributes this fragment to the "Cutter of *IG* II[2] 913," active between 210/9 and 171/70 B.C.[102]

This is part of the second decree of a prytany inscription (for the scheme, see *Agora* XV, pp. 9–10), followed by a list of *prytaneis.*

93 Fragment from the conclusion of a decree — Fig. 93

I 4427. A fragment of a stele of bluish, micaceous Pentelic marble found on January 22, 1937, over the Eleusinion (T–U 20), in a modern house wall. The tooth-dressed right side and flat, rough-picked back are preserved. There is a vertical, uninscribed space of 0.18 below the last inscribed line.

H. 0.27, W. 0.125, Th. 0.118; L.H. 0.006–0.007; non-stoich.? vert. 0.009, horizontal spacing ca. 0.004–0.005.

Ca. 210–170 B.C.? — Non-stoich.? 43–45

[- -]
[- - - τὸν γραμματέα τὸν κατὰ πρυτανείαν ἐν σ]τ̣ή[ληι λι]-
[θίνηι καὶ στῆσαι ἐν ἀκροπόλει· εἰς δὲ τὴν ἀνα]γραφὴν κα[ὶ]
[τὴν ἀνάθεσιν τῆς στήλης μερίσαι τὸν τα]μ̣ίαν τῶν στρ[α]-
[τιωτικῶν τὸ γενόμενον ἀνάλωμα] *vacat*

102. *ALC,* pp. 71–79; description of lettering, pp. 71–73; photograph, p. 72, fig. 6.

Figure 92 *(above)*. Fragment from the conclusion of a prytany decree, followed by a list of names of councillors (92)

Figure 93 *(right)*. Fragment from the conclusion of a decree (93)

Line 1: The bases of tau and of the verticals of eta survive above the phi and eta of line 2.

Line 3: The third and fourth diagonals of mu survive at the left edge.

Tracy attributes this document to the "Cutter of *IG* II^2 913."[103]

94 Fragment of a decree Fig. 94

I 4662. A fragment of a stele of gray-blue marble, streaked with white and probably Hymettian, discovered on April 3, 1937, in the area south of the Eleusinion (N–Q 12–14), in a marble dump. It is broken all around and on the back.

H. 0.136, W. 0.16, Th. 0.09; L.H. 0.004–0.005; non-stoich. vert. 0.0085.

103. See n. 102, above. Tracy comments *(per ep.)*: "the blank space along the right edge below the final lines of the decree suggests that this is a fragment of a text granting honors to an individual, perhaps, for example, a decree granting citizenship. There would have been room for a single incised crown (now lost) to the left."

Figure 94. Fragment of a decree (94)

Ca. 203–163 B.C.? Non-stoich.

[- -]
[- - - - - - - - . . . .ca. 9. . . .]ΝΕΛ[- -]
[- - - - - - - - . . .ca. 7. . . εὐ]νοια[- -]
[- - - - - - - - . . .ca. 7. . .]ΔΟΝΙΩΝ̣[- -]
[- - - - - - - - . . .ca. 7. . .]ΝΑΙ τῶι [.]ΝΑ̣Ι̣[- - - - - - - - - - - - - - - - - -]
[- - - - - - - - - . . . . σε]σωι{μη}μένων̣ [- - - - - - - - - - - - - - - - - -]
[- - - - - - - - - . . . .] π̣ριαμένου θε[- - - - - - - - - - - - - - - - - - - -]
[- - - - - - - σωμ]ά̣τω⟦ν⟧ ἀποδράντ̣[ων - - - - - - - - - - - - - - - -]
[- - - - - - - - . . .] πό<λ>εων καὶ ἐθν̣[ῶν - - - - - - - - - - - - - - - -]
[- - - - - - - - . . ἐ]κ̣λαμ⟦β⟧άνοντ[α? - - - - - - - - - - - - - - - - - - -]
[- - - - - - - - . . .]Ι̣ΔΗ τῶι ΔΕΛ̣[- -]
[- - - - - - - - . . .]ΘΑΙΑ⟦Ε⟧ΥΘ[- -]
[- - - - - - - - . .]ΩΙΤΟΥΛ̣[- -]
[- - - - - - - .]Τ̣ΕΡΑΝ̣[- -]
[- - - - - - - - . .]Θ̣Η̣[- -]
[- -]

Line 3: The lower part of the first vertical and perhaps the top of the diagonal of nu survive.

Line 4: At the right edge, nu is followed by the apex of a triangular letter and the top of a vertical.

Line 5: The mason has inscribed two extra letters, mu-eta or eta-mu, in the middle of this word.

Line 6: The lower part of the second vertical of pi survives.

Line 7: In the first stoichos the base of the right diagonal of alpha survives; the first nu is much larger than other nus on this stone and is a correction of a mistake:

epsilon may have been inscribed here first; at the right edge, nu is barely visible in the abrasion, and is followed by the left tip of the horizontal of tau.

Line 8: Delta has been inscribed instead of lambda.

Line 9: The tips of the diagonals of kappa survive in the first stoichos; the large and awkward beta is a correction for the epsilon that was first inscribed here.

Line 10: The apex of a triangular letter follows the epsilon.

Line 11: After the second alpha faint marks suggest that an iota was first inscribed here and later corrected to epsilon: the space between alpha and upsilon is too narrow for a regular epsilon.

Line 12: The apex of a triangular letter is visible in the break at the right.

Line 13: The right tip of the horizontal of tau and the top left corner of nu survive.

Line 14: The upper curve of a circular letter and the tops of two verticals are preserved.

The hand, notably the shapes of alpha, epsilon, nu, pi, rho, and omega, may be in the style of the "Cutter of Agora I 656 + 6355."[104] The mason has a tendency to place a central dot in circular letters such as the omicron of line 7 and the omegas of lines 7 and 10.

Line 1: [τῶ]ν Ἑλ[λήνων]?

Line 5: Cf. *IG* II^2 435, lines 10–11.

Line 7: Cf. *IG* II^2 584, lines 8 and 12.

Line 8: Cf. *SEG* XXXVII 92, lines 19–20.[105] Another version of this phrase may appear in **98**, below.

Line 12: [ἐν τῶι ἱερ]ῶι τοῦ [- - -]?

Line 13: [τὴν δὲ ἕ]τ̣εραν̣ [ἐν - - -]?

Figure 95. Fragment of a decree (95)

95 Fragment of a decree Fig. 95

I 4667. A fragment of a stele of pale gray, white-flecked Hymettian marble discovered on April 3, 1937, north of Klepsydra (T 25), in a modern context. It is broken all around; the rough-picked back may be original, but its treatment is not typical of its period.

104. See n. 96, above.

105. *SEG* XXXVII 92, lines 19–20 = *IG* II^2 898+; for the addition to this of I 7197 + 7199, see Habicht 1987.

H. 0.082, W. 0.088, Th. 0.075; L.H. 0.005 (lines 1–2), 0.006 (lines 3–6); non-stoich. vert. 0.01 (lines 1–2), 0.012 (lines 3–6).

Ca. 203–163 B.C.? Non-stoich.

[- -]
[- - - - - . . .ca. 7. . . .]ΛΑΒ[- - - - - - - - - - - - - - - -]
[- - - - - . .ca. 5. .]Α̣ΝΤΟΙΣΑ̣[- - - - - - - - - - - - - -]
[- - - - - . . σ]κευάζων [- - - - - - - - - - - - - - -]
[- - - - - . .] μετὰ ταῦτα [- - - - - - - - - - - - - - -]
[- - - - - .]ΝΟΣΛΕΙΠ̣[- - - - - - - - - - - - - - - - -]
[- - - - -]ΔΗΜΟΝΚΑ̣[- - - - - - - - - - - - - - - - -]
[- -]

Line 1: The lower halves of these letters survive.

Line 2: The base of a right diagonal survives in the first stoichos; at the right edge the base of a left diagonal is preserved.

Line 5: The vertical and part of the horizontal of a pi or gamma survive.

Line 6: The apex of a triangular letter is preserved at the right edge.

I believe that the hand is that of the "Cutter of Agora I 656 + 6355."[106] Note the shapes of alpha, epsilon, mu, nu, omicron, sigma, upsilon, and omega, all of which are characteristic of this mason's work.

Figure 96. Fragment of a decree (96)

96 Fragment of a decree Fig. 96

I 2416. The upper right corner of a pedimental stele of pale gray, white-flecked Hymettian marble found on February 14, 1935, west of the Tholos (F 12), in a Late Roman context. The right side, top, and back are preserved.

H. 0.143 (molding 0.04, taenia 0.02, pediment 0.06), W. 0.086, Th. 0.044 (projection of molding 0.02); L.H. 0.004–0.005; non-stoich.? vert. 0.0065 (horizontal spacing 0.0015; three letters occupy a space of ca. 0.015).

Ca. 203–163 B.C.? Non-stoich.?

[- - - - - - - - - - - - - - -]Ρ̣ΩΝΥ
[- - - - - - - - - - - - - - - . .]ΑΔ̣
[- - - - - - - - - - - - - - - - - -]

Line 1: The top of the vertical and most of the loop of rho survive; uncut space below the loop indicates that this is not a beta.

Line 2: The apex and part of the crossbar of alpha survive, followed by the left diagonal of a triangular letter in the break at right.

I believe that this fragment may be in the style of the "Cutter of Agora I 656 + 6355."[107] Note the alpha with slightly curving crossbar; the nu, whose second vertical extends above the line; the rho, whose loop is made from a series of straight lines; the tall, wide, slightly unbalanced upsilon; and the horseshoe-shaped omega, lacking finials.

The thickness of the stele, if the back is original, argues against an interpretation of this as a decree of the state, since it seems to require a very short line.[108] Perhaps, therefore, this is a decree of a phyle, or, less likely, of a deme or other body, not of the State; the possible name in line 1 would then be that of an orator or an honorand.

106. See n. 96, above.

107. See n. 96, above.

108. According to Dow's Formula; see n. 46, above. This would give a width of ca. 0.19, sufficient for ca. 20 letters.

Figure 97. Fragment of an honorific decree (97)

97 Fragment of an honorific decree Fig. 97

I 4483. A fragment of a stele of micaceous Pentelic marble discovered on February 2, 1937, in the area west of the Stoa of Attalos (O–P 8–9), in a pile of marble. It is broken all around, but part of the rough-picked back may survive.

H. 0.081, W. 0.096, Th. 0.14; L.H. 0.006; non-stoich. vert. 0.0115.

Before the mid-2nd century B.C.? Non-stoich.

[- -]
[- - - - - . . . .ca. 9. . . .] κ̣α̣ὶ̣ [- -]
[- - - - - .] κ̣α̣ὶ̣ ἀναγορεῦ[σαι τὸν στέφανον - - - - - - - - - - - - - - -]
[- - - - -]Ṇ ΑΙΣ μὲν Διο[νυσίων -]
[- - - - - .]α̣ίων καὶ Ἐλε[υσινίων -]
[- - - - - . .]Ι̣ΘΟΥ̣Ε̣ΣΤΕΦ̣[- -]
[- - - - - . . .]Σ̣Ε̣ΩΣΕ[- -]
[- - - - - . .ca. 5. .]ΣΑ[- -]
[- -]

Line 1: The tip of the lower diagonal of kappa and the bases of the diagonals of alpha and the base of iota survive.

Line 2: The lower halves of kappa and alpha and the base of iota are preserved.

Line 3: The top of a vertical survives in the abrasion in the first stoichos.

Line 4: The apex of the first alpha is preserved.

Line 5: Most of this line is heavily abraded, but parts or outlines of letters survive: the tops of a vertical, of the upper curve and central dot of theta, the upper two-thirds of omicron, the tips of the diagonals of upsilon, the vertical of epsilon, the outlines of sigma, tau, and epsilon, and the base of the vertical of phi.

Line 6: The upper diagonal of sigma and the tips of the horizontals of epsilon survive in the first two stoichoi.

The untidiness and inconsistency of the letter shapes suggest the first half of the 2nd century B.C.

Line 4: [Παναθην]α̣ίων?

Line 6: [τῆς ἀναγορεύ]σ̣ε̣ως ἐ[πιμεληθῆναι τοὺς στρατηγοὺς - -]? Cf. *IG* II² 925, line 3, as it is restored by Osborne.[109]

98 Fragment of a decree (reaffirming a grant of citizenship?) Fig. 98

I 6752. A fragment of a stele of gray Hymettian marble, with white flecks, found on April 24, 1956, on the lower slopes of the Hill of the Nymphs (A–B 16–17), among marbles from the demolition of modern house walls. The rough-picked back may be original, but, if so, is exceptionally thin; thus, the original stele may have been cut back for use as a revetment slab.

H. 0.12, W. 0.102, Th. 0.07; L.H. 0.006–0.009 (lines 1–5), 0.006–0.007 (lines 6–7); non-stoich. vert. 0.015.

Before the mid-2nd century B.C.? Non-stoich.

[- -]
[- - - - . . . .]ΤΟΤΕΙ̣[- -]
[- - - - . .]ΑΙΠΟΛΙΤΕ[- -]
[- - - - .]ΕΛΕΙΑΝΚ[- -]

109. *Naturalization* I, pp. 217–218, D104, and II, p. 191 (cf. also D105, lines 15–16, for the same clause).

Figure 98. Fragment of a decree (reaffirming a grant of citizenship?) (98)

[- - - -]ΓΟΝΟΙΣΕΙΣ[- -]
[- - - -]Ν δὲ ΑΥΤ̣[- -]
[- - - - .]ΑΙΕΙΡ[- -]
[- - - - . . .]Τ̣[- -]
[- -]

Line 1: The base of a vertical is preserved at the right edge.

Line 4: The upper apex of sigma survives at the right edge.

Line 7: The horizontal and part of the vertical of tau survive, below the epsilon and the iota of line 6.

The hand is undistinguished and extremely difficult to identify. It seems most appropriate to the first half of the 2nd century B.C. Note the inconsistent use and placing of serifs, the alphas with straight horizontals, and the tendency for letter strokes to curve slightly.

Line 2: [κ]αὶ πολιτε[ίαν - -]?

Line 4: [προ]γ̣όνοις or [ἐκ]γόνοις?

Line 5: [τῶ]ν δὲ αὐτ̣[ονόμων ἐθνῶν]? Cf. *SEG* XXXVII 92, lines 19–20: ἐκ τῶν αὐτονόμων ἐθνῶν καὶ τῶν δημοκρατου[μένων] πόλεων. See also **94**, above, line 8, for a similar phrase.

Line 6: [κ]αὶ εἰρ[ήνης γενομένης]?

Line 7: [ἀγαθεῖ] τ̣[ύχει δεδόχθαι τεῖ βουλεῖ κτλ.]?

99 Fragment of a decree — Fig. 99

I 2011. A fragment of a stele of micaceous Pentelic marble discovered on May 29, 1934, in the west-central area of the Market Square (G–I 10–14), in a marble dump. The stipple-dressed left side is preserved. The smooth flat back may also be original, but since the face seems to have been trimmed flat by subsequent reworking, in which all traces of letters on the right half of the stone have been erased, it is possible that the back, too, has been reworked. What survives of the original face is much abraded.

H. 0.17, W. 0.165, Th. 0.085; L.H. 0.005–0.006; non-stoich. vert. 0.009.

Figure 99. Fragment of a decree (99)

Mid-2nd century B.C.? Non-stoich.

[- -]
[.]Ι̣[- -]
Ω[. .]ΞΕ[.]Ι̣[- -]
ΑΛΛΑ[. .]Ρ̣[.]ΙΟΣ[. .]ΡΟΣ[- -]
ΛΟΥΤΗΚ[- - - - - - - - - - - - - - - - - - - τὰ μὲν ἄλλα καθ]-
ἅ̣περ τ[ε]ῖ β̣[ο]υ[λ]ε[ῖ -]
ΟΝΘΕΡ̣[- -]
[.]Σ̣[- -]
[.]Μ̣[.]Ε[- -]
ΣΑΜΕΝ[.]Ν[. . .] Ἐλευ[σι]νι[- - - - - - - - - - - - - - - - - -]
ΤΑΚΕΙ[. . ca. 5 . .]ΑΓ̣ΡΙΔẠΠΑΤ[- - - - - - - - - - - - - - - - - - - -]
Πειραι[έ]ων [.]Σ[. . .]ΙΕΚ[- -]
τῶι δή[μωι] Ο[.]Σ[.]ΚΡΙΤ[- - - - - - - - - - - - - - - - - - - -]
ἀπέγραψ̣εν Εὐκλ[- -]
[.]ΩΡΟΥ[.]ΑΤΟΙΣ[- -]
[. .]ΟΜΕΝΟΣΟΤ[- -]
[- ca. 3 -]ΤΟΥΣΟ[- -]
[- - ca. 6 - -]Ι̣Ι̣[- -]
[- - ca. 6 - -]Ο̣[- -]
[- -]

The letters are very faint, even on the less-worn left part of the face.
Line 1: The base of a vertical is visible in the second stoichos.

Line 2: The lower two-thirds of a vertical survive to left of and above the rho of line 3.

Line 4: The diagonals of a triangular letter are visible in the first stoichos.

Line 5: The top of the vertical and upper loop of beta survive.

Line 6: The top of the vertical and loop of rho or beta is visible.

Line 7: In the second stoichos the lower two diagonals of sigma survive.

Line 8: In the second stoichos the diagonals of a triangular letter are visible, so steep that they may belong to a mu, rather than to an alpha, delta, or lambda.

Line 10: In the eleventh stoichos, below the second epsilon of line 9, the apex of a triangular letter survives, followed by a gamma; below and to the right of the upsilon of line 9 the apex of a triangular letter is visible.

Line 17: Below the upsilon and sigma of line 16 the shafts of two verticals are visible, but there is no trace of anything between them, so I print them as parts of separate letters.

Line 18: Below the verticals of line 17 the upper curve of a circular letter survives.

The lettering is characteristic of the mid-2nd century B.C.

100 Fragment of a decree Fig. 100

I 4889. A fragment of a stele of badly eroded and sugary Pentelic marble tending to flake along the lines of foliation, which are diagonal from

Figure 100. Fragment of a decree (100)

top left to bottom right rear; it was discovered on May 23, 1937, over the west end of the Temple of Ares (J 7), in a Byzantine wall. It is broken all around and on the back.

H. 0.24, W. 0.185, Th. 0.05; L.H. 0.008–0.009 (lines 1–2), 0.006 (lines 3–5); non-stoich. vert. 0.014.

End of 2nd century B.C.? Non-stoich.

[ἐπὶ - - - - - ἄρχοντος, ἐπὶ τῆ]ς Ἐρεχθ̣[είδος - - - - - πρυτανείας, ἧι -]
[- - - - - - - - - - - - - - . .ca. 5. .]Ι̣ΣΤΩΝ[- - - - - - ἐγραμμάτευεν, - - - - - - - -]
[- - - - - - - - - - - - - - τῆς πρ]υ̣τανε[ίας -]
[- - - - - - - - - - - - - - - . . . . τῶ]ν προ[έδρων ἐπεψήφιζεν - - - - - - - - - - -]
[- - - - - - - - - - - - - - - . . .ca. 7. . .]ο̣ε[- -]
[- -]

Line 1: The abrasion at the right edge preserves the upper curve of theta.

Line 2: A vertical stroke survives below the sigma of line 1; after this is the outline of a heavily abraded sigma.

Line 3: The right diagonal of upsilon is preserved.

Line 5: The outlines of these letters survive.

The lettering is characteristic of the late 2nd century B.C., with very pronounced serifs.

REFERENCES

AAM = S. V. Tracy, *Athens and Macedon: Attic Letter-Cutters of 300 to 229 B.C.* (Hellenistic Culture and Society 38), Berkeley 2003.

ADT = S. V. Tracy, *Athenian Democracy in Transition: Attic Letter-Cutters of 340 to 290 B.C.* (Hellenistic Culture and Society 20), Berkeley 1995.

Agora = *The Athenian Agora. Results of Excavations Conducted by the American School of Classical Studies at Athens,* Princeton

III = R. E. Wycherley, *Literary and Epigraphical Testimonia,* 1957.

XV = B. D. Meritt and J. S. Traill, *Inscriptions: The Athenian Councillors,* 1974.

XVI = A. G. Woodhead, *Inscriptions: The Decrees,* 1997.

ALC = S. V. Tracy, *Attic Letter-Cutters of 229 to 86 B.C.* (Hellenistic Culture and Society 6), Berkeley 1990.

Clinton, K. 1980. "A Law in the City Eleusinion Concerning the Mysteries," *Hesperia* 29, pp. 258–288.

Culasso Gastaldi, E. 2004. *Le prossenie ateniesi del IV secolo a.C.,* Alessandria.

Dow, S. 1942. Rev. of B. D. Meritt, *Epigraphica Attica,* in *CP* 37, pp. 323–328.

———. 1963. "The Preambles of Athenian Decrees Containing Lists of *Symproedroi,*" *Hesperia* 32, pp. 335–365.

Ferguson, W. S. 1948. "Demetrius Poliorcetes and the Hellenic League," *Hesperia* 17, pp. 112–136.

Habicht, C. 1987. "The Role of Athens in the Reorganization of the Delphic Amphictiony after 189 B.C.," *Hesperia* 56, pp. 59–71.

———. 1990. "Zum Texte eines athenischen Volksbeschlusses von 304/3 v. Chr. (*SEG* XXX, 69)," *Hesperia* 59, pp. 463–466.

Henry, A. S. 1983. *Honours and Privileges in Athenian Decrees: The Principal Formulae of Athenian Honorary Decrees* (Subsidia epigraphica 10), Hildesheim.

———. 1984. "Athenian Financial Offiicials after 303 B.C.," *Chiron* 14, pp. 49–92.

———. 2002. "The Athenian State Secretariat and Provisions for Publishing and Erecting Decrees," *Hesperia* 71, pp. 91–118.

Lambert, S. D. 2001a. "Fragmente athenischer Ehrendekrete aus der Zeit des Lamischen Krieges (zu *Ag.* XVI 94 und *IG* II^2 292)," *ZPE* 136, pp. 65–70.

———. 2001b. "The Only Extant Decree of Demosthenes," *ZPE* 137, pp. 55–68.

———. 2004. "Athenian State Laws and Decrees 352/1–322/1 I: Decrees Honouring Athenians," *ZPE* 150, pp. 85–111.

———. 2005. "Athenian State Laws and Decrees 352/1–322/1 II: Religious Regulations," *ZPE* 154, pp. 125–159.

Lawton, C. L. 1995. *Attic Document Reliefs: Art and Politics in Ancient Athens* (Oxford Monographs on Classical Archaeology), Oxford.

LGPN II = M. J. Osborne and S. G. Byrne, *A Lexicon of Greek Personal Names* II: *Attica,* Oxford 1994.

Maier, F. G. 1959. *Griechische Mauerbauinschriften* I: *Texte und Kommentare,* Heidelberg.
Meritt, B. D. 1933. "The Inscriptions," *Hesperia* 2, pp. 149–169.
———. 1947. "Greek Inscriptions," *Hesperia* 16, pp. 147–183.
———. 1961. *The Athenian Year* (Sather Classical Lectures 32), Berkeley.
———. 1977. "Athenian Archons 347/6–48/7 B.C.," *Historia* 26, pp. 161–191.
———. 1981. "Mid-Third Century Athenian Archons," *Hesperia* 50, pp. 78–99.
Naturalization = M. J. Osborne, *Naturalization in Athens,* Brussels
I = *A Corpus of Athenian Decrees Granting Citizenship,* 1981.
II = *Commentaries on the Decrees Granting Citizenship,* 1982.
III–IV = *The Testimonia for Grants of Citizenship; The Law and Practice of Naturalization in Athens from the Origins to the Roman Period,* 1983.
Oliver, J. H. 1935. "Greek Inscriptions," *Hesperia* 4, pp. 1–70.
Osborne, M. J. 1989. "The Chronology of Athens in the Mid-Third Century B.C.," *ZPE* 78, pp. 209–242.
———. 2000. "Philinos and the Athenian Archons of the 250s B.C.," in *Polis and Politics: Studies in Ancient Greek History. Presented to Mogens Herman Hansen on His Sixtieth Birthday, August 20, 2000,* ed. P. Flensted-Jensen, T. H. Nielsen, and L. Rubenstein, Copenhagen, pp. 507–520.
Pečírka, J. 1966. *The Formula for the Grant of Enktesis in Attic Inscriptions,* Prague.
Pritchett, W. K., and B. D. Meritt. 1940. *The Chronology of Hellenistic Athens,* Cambridge, Mass.
Reinmuth, O. W. 1971. *The Ephebic Inscriptions of the Fourth Century B.C.* (*Mnemosyne* Suppl. 40), Leiden.
Schweigert, E. 1939. "Greek Inscriptions (1–13)," *Hesperia* 8, pp. 1–47.
———. 1940. "Greek Inscriptions," *Hesperia* 9, pp. 309–357.
Schwenk, C. J. 1985. *Athens in the Age of Alexander: The Dated Laws and Decrees of "the Lykourgan Era" 338–322 B.C.,* Chicago.
Stroud, R. S. 1971. "Inscriptions from the North Slope of the Acropolis, I," *Hesperia* 40, pp. 146–204.
Threatte, L. 1980. *The Grammar of Attic Inscriptions* I: *Phonology,* Berlin.
Tracy, S. V. 1973. "Identifying Epigraphical Hands, II," *GRBS* 14, pp. 189–195.
———. 1988. "Two Attic Letter Cutters of the Third Century: 286/5–235/4 B.C.," *Hesperia* 57, pp. 303–322.
Walbank, M. B. 1986. "Athens and Stymphalos: *IG* II[2], 144+," *Hesperia* 55, pp. 319–354.
———. 1990. "Notes on Attic Decrees," *BSA* 85, pp. 435–447.
———. 2002. "Notes on Attic Decrees," *ZPE* 139, pp. 61–65.
Woodhead, A. G. 1957. "Greek Inscriptions," *Hesperia* 26, pp. 221–236.
———. 1960. "Greek Inscriptions," *Hesperia* 29, pp. 78–86.

CONCORDANCE

Epigraphical Museum Inventory Numbers

Inv. No.	*Cat. No.*	*Inv. No.*	*Cat. No.*
2459	see **15**	7157	see **44**
2613	see **28**	7218	see **14**
2624	see **1**	7221	see **25**
2707	see **2**	7284	see **31**
6881	see **1**	7325	see **41**
6881a	see **1**	7397	see **67**
7068	see **54**	7449 + 7455	see **81**
7077	see **15**	10396	see **30**
7136	see **14**	12823	see **6**
7147–7151	see **15**	12917	see **1**

Agora Inventory Numbers

Inv. No.	*Cat. No.*	*Inv. No.*	*Cat. No.*
I 15	see **68**	I 2025	see **5**
I 96	see **68**	I 2239	**21**
I 707	see **36**	I 2266	**63**, fr. *a*
I 794	**22**	I 2416	**96**
I 935	**81**	I 2581	**39**
I 970	**11**	I 2665	**92**
I 978b	**52**	I 2721	**73**
I 1083	**85**	I 2747a	**70**
I 1086	**65**	I 2747b	**71**
I 1363	**72**	I 2764	**37**
I 1425	**33**	I 2767	see **57**
I 1449	**86**	I 2805	**25**
I 1644	**31**	I 2835	**56**
I 1904	**67**	I 2925	**5**, fr. *d*
I 1983	**79**	I 3023	**19**
I 2011	**99**	I 3058	**3**

Inv. No.	*Cat. No.*	*Inv. No.*	*Cat. No.*
I 3063	**17**	I 5317	**74**
I 3211	**55**	I 5327	see **82**
I 3237	**89**	I 5351	see **4**
I 3293	**58**	I 5361	**59**
I 3433	**49**	I 5364	**77**
I 3510	**6**	I 5368	**2**
I 3666	**9**	I 5391	**75**
I 3688	**68**	I 5405	**4**
I 3793	**45**	I 5491	**60**
I 3836	**32**	I 5492	**41**
I 3843	see **30**	I 5500	**16**
I 3858	**46**	I 5501	**13**
I 4113	see **2**	I 5505	**57**
I 4260	see **82**	I 5521	**10**
I 4265	**12**	I 5627	**36**
I 4427	**93**	I 5642	**20**
I 4483	**97**	I 5707	**26**, fr. *b*
I 4484	**38**	I 5709	see **50**
I 4491	**43**	I 5747	**76**
I 4510a	**5**, fr. *b*	I 5752	**80**
I 4510b	**5**, fr. *c*	I 5767	**84**
I 4524	**27**	I 5771	**51**
I 4530	**61**	I 5778	**26**, fr. *a*
I 4533	**35**	I 5813	**78**
I 4544	**30**	I 5823	**8**, fr. *a*
I 4545	**48**	I 5824	see **35**
I 4648	**53**	I 5838	**29**, fr. *a*
I 4662	**94**	I 5848	**28**
I 4664	**15**	I 5884	see **48**
I 4667	**95**	I 5894	**34**
I 4740	**66**	I 6065	**90**
I 4855	**88**	I 6246	**44**
I 4889	**100**	I 6306	**91**
I 4896	**42**	I 6324	**40**
I 4902c	**23**, fr. *a*	I 6384	**5**, fr. *a*
I 4902d	**23**, fr. *b*	I 6397	**1**
I 4948	**69**	I 6409	**83**
I 4955	**18**	I 6416	**50**
I 4968	**62**	I 6487	**8**, fr. *b*
I 4981	**54**	I 6582	**47**
I 4982	**24**	I 6752	**98**
I 4985	see **4**	I 6759	**82**
I 5049	**64**	I 6777	**29**, fr. *b*
I 5069	**63**, fr. *b*	I 6868	**7**
I 5171	**87**	I 7197	see **94**
I 5280	**14**	I 7199	see **94**

INDEXES

NAMES OF MEN AND WOMEN

This index is organized on the model of *Agora* XVI: "In the alphabetizing of multiple entries of the same name, simple names come first. Then follow simple names with some qualification (e.g., 'father of'). Next come names with patronymic but no demotic, then names with demotics (in the alphabetical order of these latter and whether or not a patronymic is included), and finally names of non-Athenians with their ethnics on the same principle. Occasionally an evident or possible family relationship has been more easily noted by a variation from the strict application of this formula. Restorations have for the most part been repeated as they appear in the texts, but the names of archons are always entered in their complete form irrespective of any restored element."[1]

1. *Agora* XVI, p. 506.

KINGS, EMPERORS, AND THEIR FAMILIES

THE ATHENIAN PHYLAI

DEMES AND OTHER SOCIAL GROUPS

BUILDINGS AND LOCATIONS IN ATHENS AND ATTICA

PEOPLES AND PLACES BEYOND ATTICA

THE ATHENIAN MONTHS

GODS, HEROES, AND FESTIVALS

SIGNIFICANT THEMES AND FORMULAIC PHRASES

PUBLICATIONS CITED

Inscriptiones graecae II

Inscriptiones graecae II² *(editio minor)*

Supplementum epigraphicum graecum

Hesperia

Other Publications